I0110520

Nuggets...Along the Way

Your difficulties are stepping stones in disguise

Autobiography
By
Venoris Patten

God is our refuge and strength, always ready to help in times of trouble". Psalm 46:1

TRUE PERSPECTIVE PUBLISHING HOUSE

i

Nuggets...Along the Way

DEDICATION

To my children, grandchildren and those to come;
I pray that my autobiography will motivate you to strive to
find your true purpose in life.

To all my siblings, their children,
relatives, friends and those who have influenced my life.

To all who seek purpose, heed Polonius' advice to his son:

"To thine own self be true,
And it must follow, as the night the day,
Thou canst not then be false to any man".

Taken from Shakespeare's Hamlet

Nuggets...Along the Way

ACKNOWLEDGEMENTS

I would like to acknowledge the many people who have impacted my life, directly or indirectly. So many ministries, groups, churches, secular organizations and even experiences have laid the groundwork, and molded me to be a "useable vessel", prayerfully, a vessel of honor.

The greatest sources of strength in my life are my testimony and my prayer life which form the basis for my book. I remember when I used to be timid and even fearful to pray, especially to pray out loud sadly thinking that I had to pray "good prayers". It was through the ministry of Pastor Dr. Owen Facey, that I finally came into an understanding of where I even fit in the body of Christ. I did not know that the Lord had put the ministry of Prayer Intersession and Encouragement in me. Thank you Pastor Facey.

Thanks to Church of God of West Broward, Ft. Lauderdale Florida. Under the leadership of Senior Pastor Dr. Reginald G. Smith and supportive First Lady Carol Smith, I was able to explore this newly found gift in establishing a Prayer Ministry. Later at Genesis Christian Fellowship (Ft.

Lauderdale), God granted me favor again to continue to lead the Prayer Ministry for two years under Senior Pastor Dr. Owen Facey.

Acknowledgements to Celebration of Praise ministry under oversight of Pastor Dr. Chris Dutruch and Prayer Ministry leader Elder JoJo Entsuah for their leadership and support. Under this leadership and in partnership with my wonderful co-intercessors, I gained added momentum in my determined effort to represent my Lord well.

I used to wonder what my ex mother-in-law found to pray about for all those long hours spent with her friends in intercession. That was many years ago. The tide has turned and I am seeing the great need to pray, pray, and pray some more. I say "thank you", because this was an example that I have referred to many times.

To my many personal prayer partners, whose faithful support helped me to weather the storms, I say thanks. Thanks to Dr Vivian Woodard, who prevailed with me last New Years Eve night, and way into the wee hours of the morning, when I thought I probably wouldn't make it. It was a great investment. To my mentor and friend, Sis

Delores Green who has put an indelible mark on my life; I am eternally grateful. She has spoken great wisdom into me. I hope that I can pass it on with even half as much grace.

I acknowledge those who volunteered to be interviewed, and others who shared their testimonies with me. I was so energized hearing what God is doing in their lives. I trust that JB, Steve and Jan, Graceann, and RS will keep ministering out of their experiences. We can only be helped by sharing with each other. Let us "give ourselves away" so God can use us.

My gratitude goes to the Central Florida Cancer Institute for their special care and consideration that went beyond the ordinary. When I lost my insurance coverage in the middle of cancer treatment, they stood with me for the long haul.

And special thanks to my Aunt Mildred whom God used to bless me beyond measure. I did not have to ask, she was right there. There is a special place for people like my aunt who live to give.

Nuggets...Along the Way

I would like to thank Margie Puckett for inviting me to write my testimony, published at www.inhisgrace365.org, which actually became the groundwork of this book. I acknowledge also Elder Sean Cort my publisher. It took a whole year after his encouragement to write a book, that this became a reality, albeit I had started journaling.

ENDORSEMENTS

"This is a book written by a woman who is transparent about her life...all the bumps and bruises. She is a testimony that trust and faith in God can see you to new levels in Christ and in your life. An inspirational and uplifting read!"

Deborah Cort

"Venoris Patten is a woman of prayer who believes God for all things. Within the pages of this book you will learn that she is a unique individual who draws strength from her transparency with you. Be prepared to be elevated in your faith."

Sean Cort-Publisher

"In *Nuggets...Along the Way*, Venoris Patten demonstrates that although life is unpredictable and full of struggles; perseverance, steadfastness and, above all trust in God will get you through any situation you may face. This book is a beacon of light for those who are searching in the dark for a sliver of hope. It's a must read!"

Marco A. Diaz

"In life you seldom find someone that has not just "talked the talk" but has literally "walked the walk". In "Nuggets...along the way" Venoris Patten systematically walks us through the journey of her life. A life that has been filled with challenges yet a life that has experienced great victories. Over the past 4 years as her Pastor I can testify that Venoris has been an individual that has tackled every challenge she faced with grace and has allowed the Lord to show her the ability to receive beauty for ashes. I highly recommend this book for those interested in coming out of their pain and entering into a life of sweet victory."

Bishop Chris Dutruch, D.Min. - Senior Pastor
Celebration of Praise

Nuggets...Along the Way

AUTOGRAPH PAGE

Autograph this book as a personal investment to yourself or the life of someone that God has put in your path on this life journey.

Nuggets...Along the Way

TABLE OF CONTENTS

Nuggets...Along the Way

INTRODUCTION

"Let us therefore fear, lest a promise being left us of entering into His rest any of you should seem to come short of" (Hebrews 4:1)

The Lord has put cautions in my life over the years and this verse was one of them. It came back to me as I was going through some difficulties. Recently I started reviewing my journal with the thought that maybe I could start writing my life's story. I turned to the verse (Heb. 4:1) and it gave me new inspiration.

I had written a prayer next to it that goes like this:

"Lord, help me to be careful that the difficulties of the present moment do not overshadow the reality of your promises and cause me to doubt. I will not trust my own efforts. Please heal my faith as I lean heavily on you and your promises. I know that you watch over your promises to bring them to pass in my life. You promised to heal me and so you will. You promised to deliver me, anoint me, and set me free and so you will. Thank you for being with me alway and so I enter into your rest." Amen.

"For all the promises of God in him are yea, and in him Amen, unto the glory of God by us" (2 Corinthians 1:20).

I am sure all of us can attest to the fact that our journey in life is complex and dynamic. Even if it appears to be dull and boring for a season, there is much going on in the mind and thoughts. There is much going on behind the scenes. We have to figure out how to make it in life. Some people express the dilemma in actions. Others are more expressive in dress or verbal expressions and yet others even choose the nonverbal route. There are yet those who dull their senses with drugs and alcohol and really live a completely "false" life. Whatever category we fall in, we share the same concerns of life.

My primary aim in writing this book is to encourage people, especially those who have difficulty accepting themselves. Love yourself, knowing that God has made you a unique being, and He loves you. Our society forces us to fit into a mold that is carved out to satisfy the norm, the majority, the affluent, the influential or some set that is "accepted". God forbid if you do not fit in. Ask the Lord to show you His purpose for your life. Success is not health, money, houses or land; although these go a long way to help in our contentment. True success is finding your God given purpose in life.

In his book, <u>The Power of Perspective</u> (Xulon Press 2009), Sean Cort included this statement:

"Purpose is not a destination reached but a series of opportunities along life's journey that present themselves for us to be in position physically, mentally, and spiritually to fulfill a need that destiny has placed before us, that will serve our fellow man and glorify God". To apply this truth to our lives goes a far way in finding real success.

Today I read again the whole book of Ecclesiastes and it captured the concerns of the writer Solomon. It stated that we are caught up in activities, plans, dreams, and goals that constantly drive us. Drives us where? Many times life forces us to start over again anyway; other times we are deceived to think we are ten steps ahead, but in terms of quality and worth we are a few steps behind if we are not walking in purpose. Is that not where most of us are today? Solomon describes it as "chasing wind" and "all is vanity". At the end of his queries, he finally concluded that the whole duty of man is to …. ***"Fear God and do His commandments" (Ecclesiastes 12:13).***

I believe we are here on this planet "to be our brother's keeper". Your strength and my weakness should compensate and compliment each other and vice versa.

However, instead of bearing each other's burdens, we start finding ways of cutting each other down. We get the crab mentality of begrudging someone else climbing the wall so we pull them down in order to get ahead. After a while, when we think we are really ahead, we get called into the office to see our boss only to find out that the boss is the one we "stepped on" in our pursuit of happiness. What a tangled web we weave?

Things like this happens everyday. As we strive for wisdom, knowledge and good understanding, let us strive to do the "humane" thing at all times. This is what will aid our progress into a meaningful and substantial life. If this becomes the hallmark of our lives, our journey then will never be as "chasing the wind" or be described as "vanity". Instead it will be intentional, meaningful and purposeful. I challenge you to "exhale" and let go of the pent-up issues of life. This serves as a giant leap into finding freedom. This verse bears repeating.

"Let us therefore fear, lest a promise being left us of entering into His rest any of you should seem to come short of" (Hebrews.4:1).

Nuggets...Along the Way

CHAPTER ONE

MY TESTIMONY

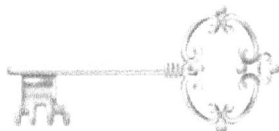

*T*he journey of my life has been nondescript in some regards, yet intentional and purposeful in other ways, especially over the most recent years.

"You are a product of your environment". This statement has been said over and over again, made popular and sounds true, but is it?

The journey I am on has cast a shadow on this trend of thought. My "growing-up" years were plagued with uncertainties and insecurities and easily I could have fallen victim to this mindset without knowing the real TRUTH of the matter. It is life changing to come to know the TRUTH and not to settle for craftily spun word put together to convince the natural mind. I am definitely not limited to just being a product of my environment. I am unique, complex, and I am "fearfully and wonderfully made".

Jesus said "I am the Way, the Truth and the Life" (John 14:6).

What God says about the matter is the only truth. There is a vast difference between the natural world and the spiritual world. Thank God for that because in accepting His Purpose for my Life, I have been transformed from a "nobody", to a woman of purpose. He has shown me that I have great significance. I now walk in purpose and every circumstance and every person along the way becomes an opportunity that God is using on my journey. That's what my Lord has done for me.

As I reflect on my life over the years, I am able to speak from a grateful heart. Thank God. I am seeing more and more how He has used even my darkest hour as a stepping stone to a higher place in Him.

At times I have felt like Hezekiah described, *"For the children are come to birth and there is no strength to bring forth" (11Kings 19:3).* After a while, the Lord started talking into my spirit about purpose and intentionality of my life. As I processed this, I became more and more accepting of who I am and where I am in my life with Him. I started journaling and as I gleaned "TRUTHS" about myself, who He is in my life, and my journey with Him, I labeled these experiences as *"Nuggets... Along the Way"*. Here are some of them.

TORCH

I remember being very dissatisfied with my life growing up. I used to wish that I was someone else and from a different home because I thought my family was too poor. My father was a hardworking farmer and my mother a faithful home maker with ten children. I always yearned for "better" and felt like I was deposited in the wrong family. My mom was the spiritual leader of the home, and "Yes" it was a home, only that I did not see the truth at that time. The enemy had deceived me and continued to do so for most of my teenage years. Little did I know that my all wise, all knowing heavenly Father had placed me in my family to witness and experience the fundamental Christian groundwork that my praying mother gave me.

I will never forget the "Torch" that mom gave me that dark morning before daylight when I had to run along a dark country road to get to my exam early in the morning. Only those who have had a taste of living without electricity can understand the emotional trauma that I experienced as I ran down the dark country road alone... And of course the wind blew out the torch. I was eleven years old.

Time and time again I have reflected on my life and on that day. In time, the Lord revealed to me a spiritual parallel. My Mom not only gave me a physical torch, but a spiritual one. She gave me the spiritual foundation that gave me light along my way. I also acknowledge that I have a great spiritual family legacy. I was rich and did not know it. I would not trade my family for any other in the world. Thank you Lord.

RIGHTS

I tend to be a "type-A" personality type. I like to see all the ducks in a row, the "t's" crossed and the "i's" dotted. I actually was proud of being this way and expected no less from others. (God is merciful. He spared my children). I ran into a decent amount of conflicts with people, both in the job arena and socially. My thought was that there are standards to maintain and we should always strive for excellence at all cost and without exception. I insisted on this because I knew that this was "RIGHT" until the Lord confronted my spirit one day.

I heard Him say, "So you are right, so what?"

I was shocked. "Eh?"

The Lord said "What are you going to do about it? What will you do with your rightness?"

I answered, "If I am right I need to speak up Lord".

The Lord responded, "Is this the time or place to implement your rights?"

I was at a loss as to what to say, so I surrendered myself and my rights to God. Now I make a conscious effort to constantly surrender. My attitude is "I give you my rights Lord. I thank you for being so patient with me".

HEALTH

Over the past year I have gotten new insight into "Purpose". I was diagnosed with breast cancer and faced surgery, radiation and chemotherapy. Just at the same time I was getting a letter from my health insurance that my policy would be expired in a short time (6 weeks I recall). Was I calm and relaxed? NO. I had issues with that. All my working life, I have had health insurance and stayed healthy but the time I needed it most I was loosing it? I had real issues with that. I said:

"Lord, what's going on?"

The Lord made me aware, not just then, but from time to time of "it" being "a set-up". Yes, whatever the "it" I was going through at that time, was a set- up. The Lord used that to show me that "when I have come to the end of my resources, His giving has only just begun". He was taking me through the school of higher learning.

The Lord has blessed me with the ability to "compartmentalize" and function well in the middle of dire situations. As I spoke with docs, therapists etc. in what seemed like robotic fashion, the Lord helped me to navigate my way through the myriad of scenarios that was a part of my care. He carried me one step at a time. Through this experience, God has proven Himself in my life not only as my lover and ever present God, but as my provider and the one that sustains me.

"And the barrel of meal wasted not, neither did the cruse of oil fail" (1Kings17:16).

He has provided for my needs through unfamiliar sources. Praise be to God who causes me to triumph.

Years ago God said to me "Be faithful and endure". I thought it was regarding issues at that time, not realizing that it is a demand on my life for the entire journey. Regardless of the storm, God is faithful. He reminded me that He has measured it against the grace He has given to me in ability and determined that it will not destroy me. Well, the onslaught has come, I have escaped, and I am being taken care of. God's plan for my life is larger than any storm. He is directing my steps towards His higher purpose and no storm will succeed in changing His plan.

In the storm we tend to fear the storm will overwhelm us. We fear we are alone in it, we fear we caused the storm, and sometimes with warped perspective, we fear the storm is here to stay.

Praise be to God, He has brought me through. I was never alone and there was a limit on the severity. He knows what we can bear. The Lord showed me also that many diseases are just the natural result of living in a fallen world, but His grace was and remains sufficient for me. I did not cause it, it was not here to stay, and God had a purpose in it.

Isaiah 43:2 says "when thou passest through the waters, I will be with thee; and through the rivers, they shall not overflow you; when thou walketh through the fire, thou shalt not be burned; neither shall the flame kindle upon you".

I had an awesome experience during my recent illness. The Lord gave me a "vision" or a "dream" of my healing (I did not know if I was really asleep or awake). There was this woman walking towards the woods with an unleashed Chihuahua angrily yapping at her heals. A few nights afterwards I continued the dream, but this time the dog was on a leash and amicably walking along with her like friends. Several nights later I saw the woman over in the opposite direction from the woods. She was praise-dancing and glorifying God! It was beautiful to see. Then I noticed that the dog was missing... As I contemplated the missing dog, the interpretation came to me that I was the woman and the dog was the cancer. It was gone. The Lord gave me this when I needed it most.

OTHER NUGGETS:

BANANA VS. ONION

Nuggets along the way came in various forms. Sometimes it was a big lesson, other times it was simply a reassuring word for the moment. I remember during one of my trials, I saw a ripe banana being peeled. I challenged the Lord. I asked Him.

"Lord, it seems like you are peeling me?"

He said "Yes, I am".

He did not say another word, but I knew what He meant. I was being processed, and I had a sense that it would be O.K.

It all seems so funny now, because after the dialogue with the Lord, I wondered why He chose a banana and not something hard, like an onion that could better stand hardship, to demonstrate the process. I am pretty sure that the Lord must have been smiling at me. In discussing this with a friend sometime afterwards, another meaning came to me.

LESSONS

- I will be processed by the peeling away of the "flesh", the things that hinder the progress of my Christian walk.

- My heart must remain soft and pliable like the ripe banana, and not get hard and unyielding like the onion

THE METALLIC MAN

The Lord reassured me of His protection while I was going through chemotherapy 6 months ago. In a vision, I was out in a field and suddenly a huge, imposing metallic man loomed up out of nowhere. I had no sense of fear, but a sense of peace that all was well. The man stood looking at me; and just as fast as he appeared to me, was as fast as the "critters" that were tormenting me retreated into the background, crying out as they went.

LESSON

The Lord made provision for my protection while I was going through my unusual journey.

I have had many storms in my life and I am sure I am not unique in this, as we live in a fallen world where people will deal with problems. I am eternally grateful for the new insights God is giving me day by day as I gain momentum in my spiritual journey. Time would not permit me to chronicle all the amazing reports and testimonies of Gods faithfulness and blessings to me. "Thanks be to God who causes me to triumph in Christ".

It's been six months since breast cancer surgery, radiation, and chemotherapy, and I am doing great. Aside from a few discomforts due to side effects of chemo and surgery, I am back to normal. I consider myself "blessed", as I acknowledge that it could have been otherwise. I count my blessings. Yet even if it was otherwise, it would not negate the blessings of God on my life.

When dire circumstances overtake us, we tend to think that God has taken His blessings away from us. That is a warped perspective of God's providence. Even Jesus was led by the Spirit into the wilderness to be tempted by the devil (Matthew 4:1). Jesus sent the apostles into storms (Matthew 8: 22-24, Mark 4:35-37, Luke8: 22-24). They found purpose in their dire situations. God's blessings on our lives do not come and go according to the changes around us, or according to how we feel about these things. We need to know who is in the "storm" with us and continue to walk in the blessing and favor that God has put on our lives.

Being a pragmatist by nature, I realize that the sudden turns, twists, and bends that are a natural part of this life can affect anyone at anytime. What I am confident in is the fact that regardless of the circumstances, my life is in God's hands. My attitude is "I will not ask for an easy life, but I will ask to be a strong person."

In conversing with a coworker this past week, I realized that the Lord has been sheltering me in a most wonderful way. Three people on the job have been struggling with the flu and other respiratory conditions over the past six weeks. Although I remain neutropenic with a low white blood cell count of 2.5(normal ranges 5 -10); in spite of many shots to boost the bone barrow production, I have been spared from getting sick. In spite of the suppressed immune system I have been able to return to some of my routines without complications. Praise be to God.

With as much as God has invested in me, giving me insight for my life and strength for the journey, I choose to follow Him. He leads and I follow. Sometimes the way is not clear, but I *"Walk by faith, and not by sight"* *(2 Corinthians 5:7).*

When darkness veils His lovely face;

I rest on His unchanging grace;

In every strong and stormy gale,

My Anchor holds, within the veil.

On Christ, the Solid Rock I stand

All other ground is sinking sand

All other ground is sinking sand.

To the person/s reading this testimony, I encourage you to seek the God who sustains in the trials of life. Regardless of where you are in life, sick or healthy, rich or poor, employed or unemployed, even on drugs or on the streets, His grace transcends barriers and avails for you. You will never learn true faith in comfortable surroundings. It is the very thing that comes to break you that God uses to propel you to a higher dimension in Him. Ask Joseph who, sold into slavery by his brothers, ultimately became governor of Egypt; ask Moses who was banished into the wilderness to starve to death. He eventually became the deliverer of Israel. You may not like the principle that God uses, but it is the same principle that He uses for all His people.

The Question is; do you really want to follow Him? If you do, then let Him use the adversities of your life as spiritual stepping stones to a higher and more triumphant place in Him.

Nuggets...Along the Way

CHAPTER TWO

WHAT DO YOU DO WHEN THE BOTTOM SHIFTS?

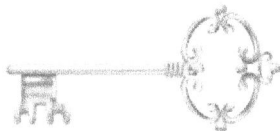

*H*ave you ever been in a place where you think "Oh Boy! It couldn't get worse?" You have used up all the money, you have no emotional reserve left, you have worked as many hours in the day as you can (bearing in mind – wisdom dictates that at some point you have to stop and rest or else you will collapse). There is still not even a dent in solving the myriad of issues that assail you. You pray for some type of reprieve, even for a little while, but instead of a "break" your husband looses his job, and the cops' escorts your son home. In other words the bottom actually has shifted.

Sometimes it gets worse before it gets better. If you are not there, you have been there or you will be there, if you hang around in this life long enough. "What do you do when the bottom shifts?" Or "what do you do when you come to the end of your rope?" I heard a preacher sum it up in few words "You tie a knot and hang on".

Putting humor aside, sometimes one gets to a place where there is nothing left to try. For the people of God, and to those who have good insight, it is still a purposeful place. Yes! You can tie that spiritual knot and let it become your lifeline. I have come to such a place a few times in my life. When I was in it, I did not understand, but now I know that it is a great place in God, "a place of surrender". God's word has given me reassurance as it tells me that *"all things work together for good to them that love God, to them who are called according to His purpose" (Romans 8:27-29)*.

NIGHTMARE.....ONLY IT WAS REAL

It was Thursday night and ten to twelve of us had Bible Study as usual and I was dropped off at my house around ten thirty or eleven. The rest of the night is recorded as the worse night of my life.

A few hours after I came home, a man broke into my house, raped me and traumatized my whole family. For days, weeks and months afterwards, I walked around in a fog. Even writing about this, years afterwards, I am tending to gloss over it fast because there are residual effects that still bother me. I do believe that God has now given me the courage and boldness to face this "demon" head-on and deal with it, once and for all. It is painful, yet liberating and I sincerely hope it will serve to set someone else free as well.

After the attack, my family and friends got me into group therapy which I could not endure at the time because it further traumatized me. It was too much to hear this woman recounting her story of what her own son had done to her. I could not stand it, so I left never to return. This was on the first day of the therapy session.

Months later I went in on a one to one session with a pastor. On the second visit, I realized that he had forgotten what I had braced myself to unburden to him the first time around. That was my final effort in seeking human help.

Many of you may have been let down by friends, coworkers, church members, and even church leaders. You may have been a player in a "horror story" involving even the pastor. We hear this over and over again. If you have been "let down" and you are hurting from such an experience, remember that the Lord Himself fore-warned us not to put trust in man.

"Don't put your confidence in powerful people; there is no help for you there" (Psalm 146:3) NLT.

Does that mean that we walk around with suspicion and doubt in relating with our brothers and sisters? No, of course not. We have an answer in God's grace. We relate with each other as openly and honestly as we can, and show grace where grace is needed, knowing that we are all imperfect beings in need of the grace of forgiveness. We look beyond our brothers/sisters and see Christ, who is the only perfect one. He is our Confidence.

"But blessed are those who trust in the Lord and have made the Lord their hope and confidence" (Jeremiah 17:7) NLT.

That assault was very debilitating. My soul was violated. In my emotions, I felt like I was being stifled and actually dying inside. At times I would ask the Lord "Why?" I wondered what is the purpose of this pain? Initially I could not even pray because I felt like the Lord had let me down. I remembered scriptures but as I used them and expected Him to honor me through them, I was left with more questions. Scriptures like, *"And if we know that He hears us, whatever we ask, we know that we have the petitions that we desire of Him" (1John 5:15)*, did not ring true anymore. I could not read the scriptures at that time because I was walking around in anger. I expected to be delivered out of the situation and it was hard to pray to the God who I thought abandoned me.

As I write this, the Lord keeps reminding me that although He did not deliver me out of the situation; yet I was delivered. He delivered me in it and is using it for further victory. My mind goes to the three Hebrew men who were thrown into the fiery furnace. He did not prevent or interrupt it, but He was in it with them. And for sure the Lord was with me. He promises that "He will never leave me nor forsake me". I believe that we are all guilty of expecting instant deliverance; and better yet, we expect that the harm must be prevented. Purpose dictates that we have to go through the process.

"Nebuchadnezzar was so furious with Shadrach, Meshach, and Abednego that his face became distorted with rage. He commanded that the furnace be heated seven times hotter than usual. [20] Then he ordered some of the strongest men of his army to bind Shadrach, Meshach, and Abednego and throw them into the blazing furnace. [21] So they tied them up and threw them into the

furnace, fully dressed in their pants, turbans, robes, and other garments. [22] And because the king, in his anger, had demanded such a hot fire in the furnace, the flames killed the soldiers as they threw the three men in. [23] So Shadrach, Meshach, and Abednego, securely tied, fell into the roaring flames.

[24] But suddenly, Nebuchadnezzar jumped up in amazement and exclaimed to his advisers, "Didn't we tie up three men and throw them into the furnace?"

"Yes, Your Majesty, we certainly did," they replied.

[2] "Look!" Nebuchadnezzar shouted. "I see four men, unbound, walking around in the fire unharmed! And the fourth looks like a god!"(Daniel 3: 19-25) NLT.

THE AFTERMATH

Over the years, I have buried my woes. I privately suffered because all these unresolved conflicts only added to my insecurities. Some loyal friends saw my plight and one in particular would read scriptures over and over to me. It was difficult to go into the sanctuary, but somehow, although I was not dressed for church, my car would end up there on Sunday mornings. I sat in the back without talking to anyone and escaped as the final "Amen" was said.

One day on the *Oprah Winfrey* show, I saw a woman whose face was scarred by acid, inflicted by her boyfriend. That day I got a visual of how my soul felt, scarred and disfigured. With this picture in my mind, I hid. My "private" side became more private and my "public" side continued to function, of course overcompensating ever so often for the imbalance in my life. I felt I had to show, if to no one else at least to myself, that I would not let anything deter me. I threw myself into work, business, and academics in which I succeeded quite well; yet there was the "inner man" to be dealt with as my soul cried for satisfaction. I was not finding real peace.

Now, when I think of that period of my life, I thank God that He carried me. I sure could not have taken care of myself. I am just amazed at His sustaining grace.

After many questions without definitive answers, I am at the place of acceptance, with insight into what He is aiming to do in my life. He is demanding higher spiritual learning. He has told me that as much as He has invested in me, He is requiring much. At this stage of my journey, God is now speaking into my Spirit confronting "Pride" in me. I am not ecstatic for "the valley of the shadows of death" experiences, but I am glad that He said He will *"be with me" (Psalm 23:4).* I am glad that even in suffering He has a plan. We can actually be set free through suffering. *"Thou has enlarged me when I was in distress" Psalm 4:1 (KJV).*

CONFRONTING PRIDE

According to *Wikipedia* "Pride is an inward directed (feeling) emotion that exemplifies either an inflated sense of one's personal status or the specific, mostly-positive emotion that is a product of praise or independent self-reflection".

According to *Dictionary.com* "Pride is a high or inordinate opinion of one's own dignity, importance, merit, or superiority, whether as cherished in the mind or as displayed in bearing, conduct, etc".

Let's see what the Bible says about Pride. This definition is according to Bakers Evangelical Dictionary.

"The Old Testament. While pride is sometimes used in the Old Testament in a positive sense (i.e., the "pride" of the land of Israel [Psalm 47:4 ; Ezek 24:21] or, God's "pride/majesty/Excellency" [Exodus 15:7 ; Job 37:4 ; Isaiah 2:10]), its negative sense predominates, occurring in sixty-one texts. "Pride" is found mainly in the prophets and the books of poetry.

The main Hebrew root is *gh* [h'aG]; the most common term is *gaon* [/a"G], which occurs a total of twenty-three times. Included are the ideas of arrogance, cynical insensitivity to the needs of others, and presumption. Pride is both a disposition/attitude and a type of conduct."

We see the effect of pride and arrogance around us everyday. Here are some results of pride as documented in the book of proverbs.

"Pride leads to disgrace, but with humility comes wisdom" (Proverbs 11:2). NLT

"Pride leads to conflict; those who take advice are wise." (Proverbs 13:10). NLT

"Pride goes before destruction, and haughtiness before a fall" (Proverbs 16:18) NLT

I never ever thought that I was any more prideful than the average person, so I thought I was O.K. In fact, the circumstances of my life dictated to me that I was a pretty humble person. I used to equate poverty or average living to humility. I realize that a vast amount of people live with this misconception as well. How foolish can we be?

The converse is likewise of concern. Many people think that progressive and influential people, especially those that are rich, cannot be humble. It seems like there are unspoken rules that support these theories.

I have come to understand that these concepts are false impositions that we place on unsuspecting people. The reality is that the poorest person can be full of pride and self-righteousness, if he/she lives under the deception of the enemy. Our own understanding can be greatly influenced by the enemy. That is why the scripture commands us to trust in the Lord and not to depend on our own thoughts.

"Trust in the LORD with all your heart; do not depend on your own understanding. Seek his will in all you do, and he will show you which path to take" (Proverbs 3:5-6) NLT.

The opposite is true that the richest person can be the most humble as he/she is led by the Spirit of God. It is a fact that there is a direct positive correlation between chasing after wealth and riches and its relationship with pride. However this is not absolute. In Matthew Chapter 19 Jesus told the story of the rich man who was inquiring about how to get to achieve eternal life. He had kept all the commandments, or so he thought. Jesus challenged him to go and sell his goods and to give the profits to the poor. He was extremely sad at this, to which Jesus responded:

Then Jesus said to his disciples, "I tell you the truth, it is very hard for a rich person to enter the Kingdom of Heaven. [24] *I'll say it again—it is easier for a camel to go through the eye of a needle than for a rich person to enter the Kingdom of God!" (Matthew 19: 23-24) NLT.*

As I gain a better understanding of spiritual matters, I see the errors of this mindset and sympathize with those who are settling for this type of thinking.

My heart goes out to Ms N. I met with her one day after I had not seen her for a while. She is the mother of an acquaintance. I greeted her warmly, but her response was somewhat aloof, to my surprise. She said;

"I didn't know that you would talk to me".

"Why would I not talk with you?" I was really uncertain what this was about.

"Well, I didn't know that you see me in your category", she responded.

I reassured her and went away puzzled. I was also irritated because I did not have the time for trivialities like that. I read into her response that I was prideful, and without clarifying it, I became defensive. The Lord slowed me down long enough to show me two things. He showed me:

- Her need for affirmation
- My pride

Obviously Ms N. had issues with insecurity, and had the view of seeing progressive people as prideful. This did not give me an excuse, as the Lord used her weakness to expose the true condition of my heart. Yes! The irritation and impatience showed where I was. Although it was not obvious to me, my defensiveness and irritation was evidence of pride that needed to be dealt with. From that day, I make a point of singling her out and affirming her, every opportunity I get. I value this lesson.

I have learnt that satan, the deceiver, will cover up the real problem and cause us to shift our attention to the less critical issues, thus we end up "majoring in the minor" things of life. That is the tool he uses to trick us to believe a lie. He did it to Adam and Eve and he continues to use the tool of deception to win on a daily basis. We need to be aware of his schemes.

Now that I understand the subtlety of pride, and the fact that the Lord is speaking to me about it in my life, my awareness is heightened. It's a waste of time for me to even bother to wonder to what degree I am prideful. The important thing is that God thinks of me enough to correct me. When the Lord speaks to me about my issues, it doesn't matter what anybody else is doing. It's about me.

The natural mind aches to be delivered from suffering, while the Spiritual Man is delivered through suffering. This is contradictory to the natural man, but the Lord has said it, so that settles it. The Lord challenged me years ago "Be faithful and endure". I have reflected on it over the years and I have taken it to heart.

"We give great honor to those who endure under suffering. For instance, you know about Job, a man of great endurance. You can see how the Lord was kind to him at the end, for the Lord is full of tenderness and mercy" (James 5:11) NLT.

DEALING WITH TURBULENCES

When there is a drastic change, it creates some type of turbulence, whether in the physical sense, mentally, emotionally, and even financially. Most people do not like change. We are sometimes afraid or apprehensive of change; however change is necessary for growth to take place. Depending on the degree of change, and the severity of the resulting turbulence, there can be varying degree of responses. Everyone responds differently and even the same person can respond in different ways at different times, depending on the circumstance or the place they are in their lives. Responses like shock, surprise, sadness, depression, acting-out, and praying are only a few of the wide array of responses there are to the changes that occur in people's lives. Depending on our background, experiences, and belief system, we embrace life differently. I have had personal experiences of many of these responses.

I remember when the Lord challenged me not to be reactive. Whatever was being said or done that affected me at the time; I would react to. I would react to how I felt without giving much thought to it, like most people generally do. It was all according to feelings. The Lord talked to me one day about reacting vs. responding. As a child of God desiring to follow the Lord, I listened and learned; "slowing down long enough to reflect on God before responding". Does this mean that I always achieve this? No! I aim to do this. I have heard it said "count to ten" before responding. It is a wise statement. Those few seconds give us a chance to at least calm down. The scriptures put it another way.

"Wherefore, my beloved brethren, let every man be swift to hear, slow to speak, slow to wrath" (James 1:19).

Another time in my life I was puzzling over the "valley experience" of life and I started challenging God. I am sure you have heard other believers talk about holding God to His promises, praying His promises back to Him, and other statements like this. It is good to do all that; however I have now come to understand that we cannot short-circuit the plan of God and the process we have to go through because they are wisely, purposely, and divinely designed. What we need is strength for the journey. God's promises will provide the strength on the way, but will not short-cut His plan. At the end of the day, God will do according to His will and purpose for our lives.

Sometimes, in spite of how we word our prayers, how long we pray, who prays over us, how we use the Word of God back to Him, the result will not be what we, the human flesh, would want. That is when we pray "Thy will be done", and take the attitude like Job.

Job said *"Though He slay me, yet will I trust in Him" (Job.13:15) KJV.*

God promises to grant us the desires of our hearts; however like all promises, it is conditional. He desires that our will be submitted to His will and our desires become His desires. To get us to that place of surrender, the human flesh, including self-will has to be killed. This process of "killing the flesh" involves pain. He knows what is best for us.

"So put to death the sinful, earthly things lurking within you. Have nothing to do with sexual immorality, impurity, lust, and evil desires. Don't be greedy, for a greedy person is an idolater, worshiping the things of this world" (Colossians 3:5)NLT.

God has been so gracious to me. I am overawed at times to think that the God of the universe, the King of Glory would consider me. This verse of a song comes to me even as I write:

How big is God; How big and wide His vast domain?

To try to tell, these lips can only start.

He's big enough to rule His mighty universe

Yet small enough to live within my heart.

This awesome God considers me enough to converse with me. I remember talking to the Lord about my hardship situation of single-parenting, the work load, and the stressors at work, trying to deal with normal behavioral issues with my children and so on. I was overwhelmed at the time. I went to bed that night and I saw a vision of a picture puzzle. I started working on it and got to the end, when I noticed that parts were missing. I was disappointed, and talked to God about it. I got no direct response.

Another time, while dealing with issues again, I had another vision of the picture puzzle. Again I worked hard at it, coming to the end and discovering again that there were parts missing. I cried to God "You give me puzzle to do with missing parts, why?" You have to understand that I, Venoris Patten, do not take kindly to leaving things undone, so it was a big concern. Once I start, I am driven. I was upset at not being able to see the end product of the puzzle.

I asked the Lord, "Where are the missing parts?"

He answered "I have the missing parts, and I will play my hand, when I will".

He revealed to me that my life is the puzzle, and there are only some parts available to me. He still has parts to align to make the complete product. Therefore, I am content to be a work in progress.

Nuggets...Along the Way

CHAPTER THREE

CONTRADICTIONS

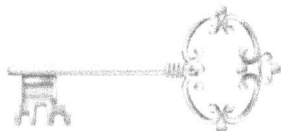

*L*ife is ever so contradictory. I read the book of Ecclesiastes again and received reinforced perspective for my life. The whole book is devoted to bringing life and the pursuit of happiness into perspective. The writer Solomon addresses the futility of all we chase after and summarizes the duty of man in one line *"fear God and do His command for this is the duty of every person" (Ecclesiastes. 12:13).* I have come to a place where I acknowledge that true satisfaction is found in finding the divine purpose for my life.

"Those who love money will never have enough. How meaningless to think that wealth brings true happiness! [11] The more you have, the more people come to help you spend it. So what good is wealth—except perhaps to watch it slip through your fingers!" (Ecclesiastes 5:10).

This is an example of futility. He suggests a solution.

"To enjoy your work and accept your lot in life—this is indeed a gift from God" (Ecclesiastes 5:19). It's all about purpose. It's all about perspective.

In our "struggles" of life, we have to accept and deal with certain realities. We have to play with the cards that we have been dealt, but pervasive among us is the fact that we all will face situations that some call "sufferings". These struggles are equalizers that serve as means to get us to acknowledge our human plight.

The common thread of humanity that allows for real kinship is not joy, but sorrow. We see this played out in disasters, for example: Hurricane Katrina and 9/11 disasters. There is a great sense of camaraderie as people look beyond their usual sphere of reference to help anyone and everyone that show some sense of need. In universal hardship everyone helps everyone. Does it have to work this way? Why do we have to suffer hardship to become soft-hearted? I believe the answer is beyond the human comprehension, but I know this statement is true "Your life will be enlarged in proportion to the degree of hardship you have endured". This for sure seems contradictory.

"Sorrowful, yet always rejoicing" (2 Corinthians 6:10)

Sorrow was beautiful, but his beauty was the beauty of the moonlight shining through the leafy branches of the trees in the woods. His gentle light made pools of silver here and there on the soft green moss of the forest floor. And when he sang, his song was like the low, sweet calls of the nightingale, and in his eyes was the unexpectant gaze of someone who has ceased to look for coming gladness. He could weep in tender sympathy with those who weep, but to rejoice with those who rejoice was unknown to him.

Joy was beautiful too, but hers was the radiant beauty of a summer morning. Her eyes still held the happy laughter of childhood, and her hair glistened with the sunshine's kiss. When she sang, her voice soared upward like a skylark's and her steps were the marks of a conqueror who has never known defeat. She could rejoice with anyone who rejoices, but to weep with those who weep was unknown to her.

Sorrow lovingly said, "We can never be united as one".

"No, never" responded Joy, with eyes misting as she spoke,

"For my path lies through the sunlit meadows;

The sweetest roses bloom when I arrive, and songbirds await my coming to sing their most joyous melodies".

"Yes and my path" said Sorrow, turning slowly away,

"Leads through the dark forest, and moonflowers which open only at night will fill my hands.

Yet the sweetest of all earthly songs – the love songs of the night, will be mine. So farewell, dear Joy, farewell".

Yet, even as Sorrow spoke, he and Joy became aware of someone standing beside them. In spite of the dim light, they sensed, a kingly Presence, and suddenly a great and holy awe overwhelmed them. They then sank to their knees before Him.

"I see Him as the King of Joy" whispered Sorrow, "For on His head are many crowns, and the nail prints in His hands and feet are the scars of a great victory. And before Him all my sorrow is melting away into deathless love and gladness. I now give myself to Him forever".

"No Sorrow", said Joy softly, "For I see Him as the King of Sorrow, and the crown on His head, is a crown of thorns, and the nail prints in His hands and feet are the scars of terrible agony. I also give myself to Him forever, for sorrow with Him must be sweeter than any joy I have ever known".

"Then we are one in Him", they cried in gladness, "for no-one but He could unite Joy and Sorrow". Therefore they walked hand in hand into the world, to follow Him through storms and sunshine, through winter's severe cold and the warmth of summer's gladness, and to be "sorrowful, yet rejoicing".

Streams in the Desert (L.B.Cowman).

PRUNING

The process of pruning that we inevitably have to endure is most difficult but very necessary. Pruning seem to be destroying the vine, and the gardener seem to be merciless in his "cutting away" of the plant. Thankfully our Heavenly Father knows how much we can bear and He is the Gardener doing the pruning. We see the evidence of the pruning in our own home gardens. After pruning, the vegetation becomes more luscious and more productive.

"I am the true grapevine, and my Father is the gardener. [2] He cuts off every branch of mine that doesn't produce fruit, and he prunes the branches that do bear fruit so they will produce even more"(John 15:1-2) NLT.

Dealing with our trials is a lifelong calling. I have read and I am applying the wisdom gleaned from my devotional reading "Streams in the Desert" by L.B Cowman (Zondervan 1997). I got it as a gift from my daughter-in-law Roxana, and it has become one of my favorite daily reading guides.

I learnt that in life, there are two ways of treating trials. One is to simply try to get out of the trial and then be thankful that it is over. The other is to recognize the trial as a challenge from God to claim a larger blessing than we have ever experienced, and to accept it with delight as an opportunity of receiving a greater measure of God's divine grace.

Even in the place of life's contradictions, one can find contentment. This contentment sometimes seems elusive. It seems like it is a secret; however it can be found. Having a sense of purpose is the first step in understanding what contentment in life is. We have to accept that tangible things will not give true satisfaction. Running after temporary pleasure will not bring fulfillment.

I walked a mile with Pleasure,

She chatted all the way;

But left me none the wiser

For all she had to say.

I walked a mile with Sorrow,

And ne'er a word said she;

But oh, the things I learnt from her

When Sorrow walked with me. <u>Robert Browning</u>

The source of true satisfaction is finding your true purpose. Paul came to that place, and concluded:

"I once thought these things were valuable, but now I consider them worthless because of what Christ has done. [8] Yes, everything else is worthless when compared with the infinite value of knowing Christ Jesus my Lord" (Phil.3:7-8).

"The secret of the Lord is with them that fear Him; and He will show them His covenant" (Psalm 25:14).

Trials of life are here to stay till the end of time, so the wise thing to do is to see the purpose in them. Yes! We change the things we can, accept those we cannot change and let them work for our advantage.

Answer this question.

Will you continue

To exhaust yourself

Battering your wings

Against immovable bars

Or will you learn

To live

Within the confines

Of your prison

And find to your surprise

That you have strength to sing

Even there? - Kathy Keay

Paul said **"I have learned the secret of being content in any and every situation…….. Whether living in plenty or in want"** (Philippians 4:12)NIV.

PROFESSIONAL ASPECTS

So we agree that life is full of contradictions. In my experience as a professional nurse for over 30 years, I have seen many things that could cause your head to spin. I'm sure many nurses can attest to this. I have seen much to cause amazement, disappointment, alarm, surprise, shock, bewilderment, even some that caused me to question purpose; just like Solomon did in the book of Ecclesiastes. At the end of his pondering, he finally described the whole path as "the futility of life". He was not saying that life was futile, but he was saying that when we miss the real purpose of our lives, we end up chasing futility. Solomon, the wisest man who ever lived, advocated for us to find purpose, and he spelled it out in Ecclesiastes 12:13-14.

"Here now is my final conclusion: Fear God and obey his commands, for this is everyone's duty. [14] God will judge us for everything we do, including every secret thing, whether good or bad".

The following scenarios show what seem like futility in some and a sense of purpose in others. If we slow down and back up from the rapid pace of life, we can always find a sense of purpose.

"And I know that whatever God does is final. Nothing can be added to it or taken from it. God's purpose is that people should fear him". (Ecclesiastes.3:14).

SCENARIO 1

Years ago, I took care of a patient DQ, who was also a physician. Usually, the staff tries to extend professional courtesy in allowing certain liberties to patients who are in the medical/nursing professions. A private room assignment for this particular patient was therefore within courtesy guidelines; however in his case it was absolutely necessary, in view of his situation.

DQ was diagnosed with colon cancer, which in those days was a death sentence, albeit very curable today depending on the staging. DQ was at end-stage and he was dying. He had a colostomy that "stunk" beyond belief, as the cancer was literally rotting within his intestines. A private room, sometimes a "status symbol", was literally an isolation room for DQ. He was very isolated. He would keep the curtains drawn all day, so the room was dark, dingy, and smelly. He had no visitors or family members and his only contacts were the nurses and allied health care workers. When we entered the room, especially after taking care of the colostomy, we had to leave right away or else we get a feeling of passing out (in spite of the strongest deodorizers).

Needles to say, DQ was not only physically isolated, but emotionally and psychologically alienated as well. I do not know how DQ was spiritually, and I have wondered about that on a few occasions. I did not ask about his spiritual life, and I have regretted it. That was a missed opportunity.

The contradiction is, DQ had lived a relatively successful life, with status, influence, and money yet he was dying without even a family member or friend around his bedside. He was left alone with literal strangers to care for him.

SCENARIO 2

BJ was in the intensive care unit, on the ventilator, with a "do not resuscitate" order written and implemented. Most people know that when this order is written, heath care workers do not do cardiopulmonary resuscitation (CPR) in the event the heart stops. What stood out in my mind about BJ was the way he died. His heart would stop for long periods of time, and then it would come back with very normal, regular rhythm. That scene kept playing out over and over for several hours.

I decided to watch what was physically happening with BJ when his heart would stop. I stood over the bed and watched. What I saw was disturbing to me. When he flat-lined, he would "grimace", like he was fearful of something, and he would relax again when his heart started beating again. I wondered about the Spirit and where it goes after death and I was compelled to pray for BJ. I do not know if he heard me or understood, because I was whispering the prayer, being quite shy about praying at that time. That scenario continued for hours before he finally died.

I do not know the outcome of BJ's journey on earth, but I know that his soul went somewhere when he left this earth. I hope he went to heaven. I did not know what caused him to be so fearful while he was dying. Sadly, he was not able to respond to me, even after I prayed for him. The scriptures admonish us to serve the Lord in our youth. There is no guarantee that there will be opportunity to honor Him later. Solomon said:

"Don't let the excitement of youth cause you to forget your Creator. Honor him in your youth before you grow old and say, "Life is not pleasant anymore" (Ecclesiastes 12:1-3) NLT.

SCENARIO 3

Nursing homes can be very depressing for the health care workers. Can you imagine the effect they have on the patients? I met MG at a nursing home years ago. The residents are usually long-term with multi-system problems, which result in very slow positive results. Most of them never go home and actually go to their eternal home from there. Basically all that the care giver does is maintenance care.

Many of these patients are lonely, and many are neglected by family members and friends. Such was MG. He was an angry man. One day, I ventured to speak to him about God. The words were hardly out of my mouth, before a long list of profanities polluted the atmosphere. He was cursing and swearing on the top of his lungs. That day I learned the full extent of MG's anger. It was very shocking to me. I literally turned around, half expecting to see fire come down from heaven to consume us.

I thank God that He is not like man who would have shut him up right there and then. God is merciful. I can just hope that MG had finally surrendered his life to God before he died. It is possible to become so hard hearted that repentance is impossible.

Jesus speaking:

"To those who listen to my teaching, more understanding will be given, and they will have an abundance of knowledge. But for those who are not listening, even what little understanding they have will be taken away from them" (Matthew 13:12) NLT.

"For the hearts of these people are hardened, and their ears cannot hear, and they have closed their eyes— so their eyes cannot see, and their ears cannot hear, and their hearts cannot understand, and they cannot turn to me and let me heal them" (Matthew 13:15) NLT.

"Their minds are full of darkness; they wander far from the life God gives because they have closed their minds and hardened their hearts against him" (Ephesians 4:18) NLT.

"The Lord isn't really being slow about his promise, as some people think. No, he is being patient for your sake. He does not want anyone to be destroyed, but wants everyone to repent. [10] But the day of the Lord will come as unexpectedly as a thief" (2 Peter 3:9) NLT.

SCENARIO 4

HM had been prepped for open heart surgery and was scheduled for later that morning. I was meeting him for the first time and he was quite apprehensive. He started asking me about the success rate of the particular surgery, and the job history of his surgeon. That particular surgeon was not one of the best; in fact he was not one most would have recommended. I had to put on my diplomatic hat really fast.

I told HM that it was always appropriate and, in fact, recommended to get a second opinion in those critical surgeries. He was very grateful, albeit very nervous.

The Lord spoke to me then.

"Pray for the man", He said.

This usually was not my first line treatment plan, so I was hesitant. Our culture has tied our hands so much in terms of faith issues, that freedom is restricted. The Lord challenged me further, and I obeyed. I pulled the curtains around us for privacy, and at that time the enemy started bombarding my mind with doubts and concerns.

"How will you pray? Will you use the name Jesus or will you say God?" satan asked.

You see HM was a Jewish man and thus the concern that I might offend him by using the name Jesus. But God gave me boldness and I prayed in the name of Jesus, just like I pray always. Harry held his head down during the prayer and at the end he agreed with me in "Amen". He looked up at me afterwards and asked me, with a very serious look.

"Are you an angel?"

Who knows, maybe God in His unlimited capacity used me in an angel capacity that day.

These and many other scenarios in my life as a Registered Nurse have helped me in gaining a sense of true perspective. My professional life has certainly factored into my growth in purpose. I have had times when I felt like walking away from my job and not return. Yet there were other times when I was overwhelmed with appreciation for the fulfillment that I have experienced as I served my patients. These scenarios that have stayed with me for all these years have obviously contributed significance and purpose to my life. I was paid to do a service, but there were many times when my experiences created a deep awareness of intentionality of a higher order. In essence I was paid double.

CHAPTER FOUR

THE PROCESS

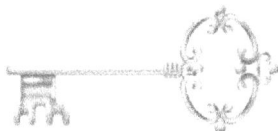

*A*s I jumped over boulders and navigated the sudden twists and turns that I have come upon on my Christian journey, I have gained great spiritual insight and gained new strength. I do daily "quiet time" with the Lord, when I read the scriptures and pray. Various people describe it differently, some say daily devotion, prayer time, and so forth. One particular segment from my devotional guide has inspired me to write this chapter.

From Streams in the Desert

"Every branch that does not bear fruit he prunes so that it will be even more fruitful (John 15:2)".

A child of God was once overwhelmed by the number of afflictions that seemed to target her. As she walked past a vineyard during the rich glow of autumn, she noticed its' untrimmed appearance and the abundance of leaves still on the vines. The ground had been overtaken by a tangle of weeds and grass, and the entire place appeared totally unkempt. While she pondered the sight, the Heavenly gardener whispered such a precious message to her that she could not help but share it.

The message was this: "My dear child, are you questioning the number of trials in your life? Remember the vineyard and learn from it. The gardener stops pruning and trimming the vine or weeding the soil only when he expects nothing more from the vine during the season. He leaves it alone, for its fruitfulness is gone and further effort now would yield no profit. In the same way, freedom from suffering, leads to uselessness. Do you now want me to stop pruning your life? Shall I leave you alone?

Then her comforted heart cried, "NO!" Homera Homer-Dixon

I welcome the pruning process in my life. I can make this statement because my God has invested divine insight into me as I go along. I have never been inclined to take the easy way out. My tendency has been to do the right thing regardless of how difficult it is. Do not peg me out to be a prude or goodie two shoe because God knows, I have done my share of mess ups. It is not that I am so good. It is because I was brought up to be so compliant which, in some ways, hurt me along the way. The draw back of that aspect of my life was that I did not explore much of what I should have explored, while I was growing up. However, I am at a good place, and God is using everything for my good and for His glory

"And we know that God causes everything to work together for the good of those who love God and are called according to his purpose for them" (Romans 8:28)NLT.

I am excited about my fractured and imperfect life. I have great expectations for what God is doing, and what He will do in my life. You may see me one day with tears running down my face, and be alarmed; and you may desire to reach out to help me. "Thank you" if you do, because we all need a helping hand at times. However tears do not deter me, disappointments do not frighten me, and whatever the roadblocks may be, they are going to be used as stepping stone to get to the next rung of the ladder.

Thank God, I am in a different place now. It excites me to experience God at work, to see His hand and to experience His presence. Unfortunately, to get to this place, I've had to go through some valley experiences. This is not what I would gladly choose for myself, but this is what the all-wise, all-knowing, ever-present God chooses for all His children. I do not understand many things. What is being developed in me is a heart of thanksgiving. I fail miserably at times and sometimes forget to be grateful, but He is still working on me.

"Acknowledge that the LORD is God!

He made us, and we are his.

We are his people, the sheep of his pasture.

4 Enter his gates with thanksgiving;

Go into his courts with praise.

Give thanks to him and praise his name.

5 For the LORD is good.

His unfailing love continues forever,

And his faithfulness continues to each generation"

(Psalm 100: 3-5) NLT.

My prayer:

Lead me; Guide me, along life's way

For if you lead me, I will not stray

Lord, let me walk, each day with thee

Lead me, Oh Lord, Lead me.

I am Lost, if you take your hand from me

I am blind without your light to see

I am putting all my trust in thee

Lead me, Oh Lord, Lead me. (Author unknown)

"God will make this happen, for he who calls you is faithful"

(1 Thessalonians.5:24)NLT.

In his book, Streams in the Desert (Zondervan 1997) L.B. Cowman included this Devotional guide:

"The Lord will fulfill His purpose for me" (Psalm 138:8).

*There is a divine mystery in suffering, one that has a strange and supernatural power and has never been completely understood by human reason. No one has ever developed a deep level of spirituality or holiness without experiencing a great deal of suffering. When a person who suffers, reaches a place where he can be calm and carefree, inwardly smiling at his own suffering, and no longer asking God to be delivered from it, then the suffering has accomplished its blessed ministry; perseverance has **"finished its work" (James 1:4)** and the* *pain of the Crucifixion has begun to weave itself into a crown.*

*At this place, persons' emotions are weaned away from other people or things, becoming deadened so that nothing can hurt, offend, hinder, or get in his way. He can now let the circumstances be what they may, and continue to seek only God and His will, with the calm assurance that He is causing everything in the universe, whether good or bad, past or present, to work, **"for the good of those who love Him" (Romans. 8:28).***

"The main thing is to suffer without becoming discouraged." Francois Fenelon

God is the Sovereign God of all events, who rules history to fulfill His purpose. What His will determines, His power carries out. No army, government, or council can stand in God's way.

ISOLATION

I do not know why the Lord uses the condition of isolation, to get His peoples attention. What I understand is that isolation can "make you or break you". In isolation, you can look down and be defeated, or look up and see that God has a purpose, even in solitude.

God isolated John to the Isles of Patmos (Revelations1). He allowed Moses to be banished into the backside of the desert, wandering for 40 years. How about Joseph who was sold into slavery, thrown into a pit, and imprisoned in Pharaoh's jail for years? Later on, John the Baptist had his share of solitude in the wilderness. Paul's, minister to the Gentile, life was full of upheavals as he provoked imprisonment, for Christ sake, on so many occasions. There were many others who had physical and emotional isolation.

They had to struggle daily because they were sent with an unpopular message to a hostile people. For years Noah looked foolish, building a boat to rescue the people from a flood, when these people did not even know what rain looked like. Job suffered agony at the city's dump, maintaining his innocence when everyone, even his wife abandoned him.

"So Satan left the LORD's presence and he struck Job with terrible boils from head to foot" (Job 2:7-9) NLT.

"Job scraped his skin with a piece of broken pottery as he sat among the ashes. ⁹ His wife said to him, "Are you still trying to maintain your integrity? Curse God and die"(Job 2:8-9) NLT.

Please know also that Jeremiah, known as "The Weeping Prophet", was not weeping because he was an emotional weakling, but he struggled daily to deal with an unrepentant, strong willed people who opposed God and His word. In spite of their rebellion, the love of God constrained Jeremiah to continue to preach to them.

Jesus, the only perfect man, also choose solitude. He would wake up early before day to pray and enquire of God. God also directed Jesus to be tempted during time of isolation. He endured, and serves as a perfect example for us. He knew the benefits of solitude.

"Then Jesus was led by the Spirit into the wilderness to be tempted there by the devil. [2] For forty days and forty nights he fasted and became very hungry". During that time the devil came and said to him, "If you are the Son of God, tell these stones to become loaves of bread"

(Matthew 4:1-3) NLT.

It seems sacrilegious to put myself in such a distinguished group. I hesitate greatly at the thought; However we are called to do even "greater works" than they. John recorded Jesus stating this.

"I tell you the truth, anyone who believes in me will do the same works I have done, and even greater works, because I am going to be with the Father" (John 14:12) NLT.

Jesus requires us to continue the work that our forefathers have founded. Just like these men of old were unique and had unique assignment, so we are called to do our individual work. Isolation or solitude takes us from the hustle and bustle of a busy life, to a place where the Holy Spirit can deal with the individual spirit. Isaiah was told to go and hide by the brook, Kerith. Here the providential Hand of God gave Elijah to eat and drink, during a time of famine. We have to be taught the "hidden side of life".

"Then the LORD said to Elijah, ³ "Go to the east and hide by Kerith Brook, near where it enters the Jordan River. ⁴ Drink from the brook and eat what the ravens bring you, for I have commanded them to bring you food" (1Kings17:3-4) NLT.

The experiences that have kept me emotionally isolated over the years were meant for evil. They were meant for evil by the enemy of my soul, whose purpose is to steal, to kill and to destroy. My Sovereign God stepped in at the appropriate time and said "Enough is Enough". He is now showing me that He is "turning what was meant for evil, for good". Jesus came that I might have life and live in abundance, so I am living abundantly.

"The thief cometh not, but for to steal, and to kill, and to destroy: I am come that they might have life, and that they might have it more abundantly" (John 10:10) KJV.

More and more, I am getting to a place of rest in Jesus. I do not want to be like that troubled lake that distorts the image of Christ. I greatly desire to reflect His beauty, so I have to come into rest in Him. In that place of rest, regardless of the storms of life, like the old seaman said, I set the ship in that certain position and stay the course.

I am reminded of the movie Twister. When the stars, Helen Hunt and Bill Paxton, were caught up in the center of the tornado, they held on and looked up. They were able to see sunbeams coming down directly on them. It was very tranquil in the center and all around was debris of all sorts. I know it is only a movie, but this graphically shows a clear picture of the peace that Jesus gives. The Lord can use anything He chooses to teach us Spiritual truths. It is possible to find peace and rest in the midst of the storms.

It is very unusual for there to be complete quiet in the soul, for God almost continually whispers to us. And whenever the sounds of the world subside in our soul, we hear the whispering of God. Yes, He continues to whisper to us, but we often do not hear Him because of the noise and distractions cause by the hurried pace of our life--- **Frederick William Faber***.*

Nuggets...Along the Way

CHAPTER FIVE

IT'S A SET-UP

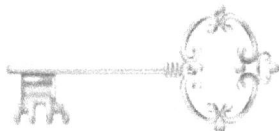

I grew up quite sheltered. This does not necessarily mean protected, but more like "with lack of exposure". I was usually the last to know anything. I was shy and unenlightened, and to some degree I remain somewhat so today. I struggled when I reached puberty, and continued to learn the "hard" way through my life. Yes! My social life was a challenge and needless to say, I did not date much. I believe I was an easy target for street-wise guys who took advantage of my naïveté on a few occasions.

ANGEL TO THE RESCUE

I was about 12 or 13 years old when, what initially started out as an innocent trip to the park, could have altered my life forever; in those days in Jamaica, as a 13 year old, I was still quite naive. My friend and I had gone to Hope Gardens which, at that time, was the largest botanical garden in the country and served as one of the main attractions on Sunday afternoons. After a while we met up with two boys, we had never seen before. We paired off and went our separate ways. Hours went by and we were oblivious of the fact that the sun was going down over the horizon and most people had left the park.

This boy and I were busy frolicking on the gradient, next to the fence of a "rich" house. We would go up the gradient and roll down to the bottom on the soft grass. This we did over and over, getting closer and closer. The next thing I knew was that we were arms in arms, cuddling and caressing like "nobody's business". I have thought about this episode from time to time, and shudder to think how my life could have been suddenly altered.

I have heard that there is nothing called a "guardian angel". We will call him a guardian angel or ministering angel or heavenly body or whatever name you can ascribe to him; what I know is that my heavenly Father sent one of them to protect me. I know he was there for me because when I least expected, there He was; a very big and imposing man standing by the fence with a huge dog. He did not say a word. His manner said it all.

"Get up and go home", his manner seemed to say to me.

We did not move right away and he continued to stand there looking at us with a challenge on his face.

"Do you dare defy me?" He seemed to say. At that time we got up and got packing. He did not change position or his gaze, but with that challenge in his eyes, he watched us walk away.

Over and over again I have reflected on this experience in my life. Although it happened so long ago, it still seems quite recent. That was one of the many lampposts that I have received to shed light on my journey along the way. I get overwhelmed with gratitude at the awesomeness of my providential God. If He had not come to my aid that day, I may have been viewed as just another number in the statistics of "wayward nonproductive bunch". I did not even know the boys last name. I shudder to think of the branding of the "loose girl" or something like that. I was not a loose girl but I was a very foolish one. I know that these are occurrences that happen on a daily basis. I also know that all people, children and adults alike, have choices to make on a daily basis. Some of our choices are good, others are bad and some mar our lives forever. I thank God that even when I had chosen foolishly, His love and mercy superseded on my behalf.

I am aware that we are in a spiritual warfare. The enemy of our souls is always setting traps for us, even from a young age. If we are not vigilant and sensitive to the strategies of the enemy, he can easily defeat us. There are times when we are unaware of others like; parents, aunts, family members or friends praying for us. In addition, our heavenly Father who is rich in mercy extends Himself on our behalf, even when we are not thinking of Him. He definitely showed me mercy that day.

As I write this, God is activating the seed of compassion that He has put in my heart for the less fortunate. The frequently used phrase "there go I, but for the grace of God" comes to my mind. I am not thinking of it lightly. In fact I just prayed:

"Lord, thank you for rescuing me that day and the many times you have rescued me since then; some I do not even remember. This one in particular is significant, because you use it to remind me of gratitude. Thank you for using it to remind me to show compassion for the "less fortunate" and the "marginalized" in our society. I pray strength and courage for all who will read this book. I pray that they will see beyond their pain and see hope in you Lord. Cause them to see that at the end of their faith they can still trust you. Let them understand that even when they cannot trace your hand, they can trust your heart. Amen!

"I pray that from his glorious, unlimited resources he will empower you with inner strength through his Spirit. [17] Then Christ will make his home in your hearts as you trust in him. Your roots will grow down into God's love and keep you strong. [18] And may you have the power to understand, as all God's people should, how wide, how long, how high, and how deep his love is. [19] May you experience the love of Christ, though it is too great to understand fully. Then you will be made complete with all the fullness of life and power that comes from God" *(Ephesians3:16-19) NLT.*

Often, we thwart the plan of God's intervention in our lives by taking up our own cause, and "striking a blow in our own defense". May God grant us the silent power and the submissive spirit to wait on Him.

"Be still in the presence of the LORD, and wait patiently for him to act" *(Psalm 37:7b) NLT.*

"So it is good to wait quietly for salvation from the LORD" *(Lamentation 3:26) NLT.*

So I pray this prayer.

"I will stay where you place me; I'll work dear Lord. Though the field be narrow and small, and the ground be neglected and stones lie thick; and there seem to be no life at all.

The Field is your own, only give me the Seed; I'll till the dry soil while I wait for the rain; and rejoice when the green blades appear; Ill work where you have put me".
(Author Unknown)

UNEXPECTED SOURCES

I met RS by what seemed coincidence. What transpired afterwards cause me to conclude that it was providential. I was the RN assigned to her son's care in the Recovery Room. I took the usual care as I did with all my post-operative patients. In this case, there were concerns in his early recovery phase. He had severe abdominal pains unrelieved by large doses of narcotics, and other symptoms indicating internal bleeding. I jumped into action doing the things that I anticipated the surgeon would do, for example: relevant blood works, abdominal binder, and "stat" call to the surgeon. As soon as was appropriate, I invited Mom in to visit her son. She came in shortly before the surgeon got there; he had been involved in another surgery.

When RS entered the recovery room, I knew she was a woman of faith, by her approach and her mannerisms. We made an instant connection. It turned out that she was an RN from a different part of the state. I extended to her profession courtesy in allowing her to stay beyond the usual limited time allowed in the recovery room. I explained in details what had happened, what had been done so far, and the plan of care. The surgeon came in at about that time, further orders were implemented and the patient subsequently transported to the surgical floor.

It turned out that the ensuing period of about 6 to 8 months were an uphill climb as RS's son continued to have problems, requiring intensive unit admissions, ventilator care, unexplained bleeding issues and infections. Through this we kept in touch via phone. During this time also, I was diagnosed with breast cancer.

During that new saga of my life, my new found friend and now prayer partner, supported me with frequent and almost daily calls, prayers on the phone, cards, words of encouragement, even surprising me with monetary gift. At the same time she was taking care of her ailing son.

The second time I met RS, I was uncertain who she was because we had met just the one time in the hospital; many months had passed. Isn't it amazing that God can bring two strangers together and a bond of kindred spirit can develop over a period of only months? It turns out that we have similar drive, determination and outlook on life. We also are a great source of encouragement to each other in ways that many others would not necessarily understand. I believe the Lord set us up on that day for the journey we had to go through. Our God is amazing.

The outcome of RS's son is a great testimony for the family. He received a kidney transplant, and with gratitude to God, he is finally living a simple and uncomplicated life with his wife and daughter. Praise God, he is now free from three-times-week hemodialysis.

I am sure we can all agree that life in general is a mystery. We try to figure it out as we go along, but we have to admit that it is beyond us. We understand some things eventually and yet other things we have to just chuck it up to mystery. The natural things of life are generally what are explainable, but there is a higher order that only those who are awakened spiritually can understand, and even then in a limited way.

"Just as you cannot understand the path of the wind or the mystery of a tiny baby growing in its mother's womb, so you cannot understand the activity of God, who does all things" (Ecclesiastes 11:5) NLT.

"No, the wisdom we speak of is the mystery of God — his plan that was previously hidden, even though he made it for our ultimate glory before the world began" (1Corinthians 2:7) NLT.

God's plan requires us to live by faith. He does not explain things to us and wait for our understanding. He gives us sufficient for us to go by and then He says to go. We are required to "walk by faith and not by sight". That means taking God at His word without fully understanding it. The mysteries of God unfold as we trust Him in our journey in life. These mysteries are so much and so deep, that we could not comprehend it all, even it was all explained to us. Take for instance the story of Lazarus.

Lazarus sisters, Mary and Martha, could not understand why Jesus was taking so long, even when they had alerted Him that Lazarus was dying. Lazarus was described as "the one who Jesus loved". They expected that Jesus would come to the aid of his friend right away. After all, everyone knew that Jesus loved Lazarus. So it was quite puzzling when the Scriptures recounted this:

"So although Jesus loved Martha, Mary, and Lazarus, ⁶ he stayed where he was for the next two days" (John 11:5-6) NLT.

This would be mind-boggling to know that your friend knows that you are very sick and dying, and does not come to visit, especially if he can do something to help you. Wouldn't it? This friend chose to delay His visit. The natural question is "what sort of love is this?" Jesus had a plan and a purpose for His delay and it's reflected in the previous verse.

"But when Jesus heard about it he said, "Lazarus's sickness will not end in death. No, it happened for the glory of God so that the Son of God will receive glory from this" (John 11:4) NLT.

Mary and Martha could not understand why Jesus did not come. In their response they sounded as if they were even accusing Him, as we do at times. Mary said, *"Lord, if only you had been here, my brother would not have died".* In this we hear the question we so often hear today, "Why?" Lord we do not understand why you took so long and why you allow such suffering and pain"? Jesus had to teach Martha, Mary and the people spiritual truths, in order for them not to "grieve as those without hope". Many times we do not understand why God deal with us the way He does.

Abraham could not understand why God asked him to sacrifice his only son either; nor could Joseph understand that God could have a purpose in his brothers selling him into slavery; why Potipher's wife told lies about him causing him to be imprisoned. Moses also was banished into the wilderness for 40 years. We may ask "what is the purpose to such suffering?" They did not understand but they had faith to believe that God had a purpose in it.

Jesus said in essence to Mary, **"You may not understand, but if you believe, you will see".** Jesus calls us to believe on His word.

Jesus responded, "Didn't I tell you that you would see God's glory if you believe?" (John 11:40) NLT.

All these men saw the glory of God worked out in their situation. Moses endured and subsequently led the deliverance of the Jews from Egypt. Joseph honored God and after many years became governor of Egypt, even saving his father and brothers from famine. Abraham's son was spared as the Lord supplied a substitute sacrifice. All these men were set-p with trials beyond the ordinary. From the natural standpoint, they were designed to fail, but God had a divine plan. "What was meant for evil turned out for good". We too are called to obey God and follow His precepts for our good. We will see our mysterious situations work out for ultimate good, even to the saving of souls.

Most of the dramas of our lives are very unreasonable and many defy logics. The day I took my son to the orthopedist turned out to be filled with surprises. My son had bumped his foot into the couch and it was now swollen, preventing him from putting shoes on. He was unable to go to school.

After x-rays were taken on him, I decided to talk to the doctor on my own account. I had been having pains in my knee, preventing me from stooping the correct way at work; the improper positioning was then affecting my back. He did x-ray of my knee also.

When the doctor came back to us, he had much to say and he said it all very briskly, as most doctors do. I was struggling to comprehend it all. He pointed it out, while showing me the x-rays:

- Your son has three fractured toes

- There is a pin in his foot

- You have a tumor in your femur

I felt like I was in a twilight zone. I went around like a robot as the front desk attendant scheduled me for a bone scan at a nearby hospital. I was also given a referral letter and a tentative appointment to an orthopedic oncologist; this is a highly specialized area of work, with only two such doctors in Florida at that time.

The ensuing months proved to be extremely challenging. The Bone scan result showed "Hot, active tumor" spelling out urgency. The insurance company gave me the worse run around; so much so that I had to threaten "to go up to Washington and camp out" before I could get to someone to really listen to me. Finally I got authorization and the Bone biopsy was done.

After the Biopsy, I was on crutches for three months. I was unable to work and I was single parenting at the time. I had made no preparation for this altered way of life, because it was an emergency, and I did not know that I would be temporarily disabled. This caused great hardship for my son and me at the time. I remember times when I would get depressed, but God in His mercy sustained me.

We weathered the storms and we are not the worse for it, but we are better having gone through. God has proven Himself to be my great sustainer. Jesus promises that He will not allow us more than we can bear, and He is true to His word.

Jesus speaking, "I had to feed you with milk, not with solid food, because you weren't ready for anything stronger. And you still aren't ready"

(1 Corinthians 3:2) NLT.

Jesus speaking, "The temptations in your life are no different from what others experience. And God is faithful. He will not allow the temptation to be more than you can stand. When you are tempted, he will show you a way out so that you can endure"

(1Corinthians 10:13) NLT.

The drama of that event played out like this. Thank God, the biopsy came back negative for cancer; however I had to follow up with x-rays twice a year for 2 years, then annually for 3 years. They were concerned that the location of the tumor could block my bone marrow production. My God is taking good care of me daily.

My son fractures were not casted, but were allowed to heal on their own, with immobilization. What became of the pin in my son's foot? It was ignored. So much was going on at the time that it got put aside. You may be thinking at this juncture, "shame on you, bad mother". To that I say I trusted God to take care of it just as trusted Him to take care of the tumor. I was somewhat uncomfortable at times, but the doctor reassured me that it was O.K. and that we should leave it alone.

The Lord used this situation to "stretch" me to a place of trust, surrender, and faith. The same faith I have to heal me of the tumor in my leg is the same faith that I extend for the healing of my son's foot. Be aware that there are thing beyond the doctor's ability, but "nothing is impossible with God".

This is what I ask of the Lord as I became aware that He was and is obviously "stretching me".

Take me higher than I've been before

Take me further, Lord I long for more

Take me deeper than I've been before

Jesus I need more, yes I long for more

"It is good for me that I have been afflicted; that I might learn thy statutes" (Psalm 119: 71) KJV.

MEANT FOR EVIL/TURNED TO GOOD

I met Steve and Jan a few years ago. I got to know them even better when I was the RN assigned to Steve after his surgery for Prostate Cancer. After his surgery, he had delays in being discharged due to complications, and was subsequently readmitted for co-morbidity issues. Steve and Jan have had their fair share of testings in life. They have had a pretty complicated life and by the grace of God, they are still alive and well to tell their story.

STEVE

- Background: catholic faith
- From alcoholic family
- Parents divorced and remarried when he was very young
- Lifestyle of his parents perpetuated into his life
- Was involved in both drugs and alcohol
- Started hard drugs use at 14 years old

- Forgot most of his teenage years because he was mostly "wasted"

- Was in a vicious cycle of life

- Had 23 "DUIs"

- Incarcerated

While Steve was incarcerated, he received a letter from a friend, introducing him to a recovery center in Lake Tahoe. He went through the recovery program and for 19 years he has been a recovering drug and alcoholic. After his incarceration he was involved in a major motor vehicle accident. At this time he rededicated his Life to the Lord and has been serving Him specifically in the area of "Overcomer's Outreach Programs".

"Overcomers Outreach" is a bridge between Alcoholic Anonymous (AA) & Narcotics Anonymous (NA) and the church. The aim of this program is to give support to those "reformer" who are struggling with self-worth. It serves as a springboard to an assurance that Christ accepts them and they are loved in spite of their past. Some people struggle because their perspective has been warped. Regardless of how much people, including the Church would reach out to them, they would not receive the love because of feelings of poor self-worth. It takes those who have been there to help them with a new reality.

JAN

- Background: Catholic

- Alcoholic home

- Grew up under domestic violence

- Sexually molested at 7 years old

- Inconsistency in her life due to divorce and remarriage in parents

- Divorce and remarriage played out in her own life

- Married an abusive, alcoholic man

- Hardships of single parenting

- Started drugs at young age

- Experienced drunkenness at age 11

- Incarcerated for drug possession

When Jan was incarcerated, she came face to face with the reality that she needed serious help. She went through a drug rehab program, during which she rededicated her life to the Lord. For 13 years, she has been drug and alcohol free and walking with the Lord. Her ministry is in the area of Encouragement in, "coming alongside those who are struggling with substance abuse".

TOGETHER

After incarceration, Jan moved into an apartment, away from her boyfriend. She met Steve, who lived in the apartment across from her. He had been in Recovery for 6 years. She invited herself along with him to an AA meeting; so in essence Steve introduced her to "Recovery". At that same time Jan rededicated her life to the Lord and they were married a year afterwards. Since then, they have been involved in Recovery Outreach. They have done jail meetings and camp-outs; all geared at giving support to recovering alcoholics and other substance abuse victims. In their ministering, they have found out that others were struggling with the same issues of self-worth that had plagued them. They have since learnt about and are implementing the Christian 12 step program called "Overcomers Outreach".

BIRTH OF THEIR MINISTRY

Obviously, Steve and Jan's life experiences have prepared them as prime candidates to deal with people struggling with addiction. They have developed the necessary sensitivity and insight to forebear in this ministry. I have observed that they are non-judgmental towards all people, and are particularly sensitive to the needs of those who seem to go back and forth as addicts tend to do.

Together they have worked for 3 years in Overcomers Outreach in Lake Tahoe, and continue to lead in this area at our home church, *Celebration of Praise (3700 south U. S. Hwy 27, Clermont, FL. 34711 # 352.394.2855)*. Under the oversight of Senior Pastor Dr. Chris Dutruch, they have established a Recovery Ministry for those with dependency issues.

God uses our brokenness for the benefit of others going through. What the enemy means for evil, God changes for good. This happens to be Jan's favorite scripture verse.

"You intended to harm me, but God intended it all for good. He brought me to this position so I could save the lives of many people" *(Genesis 20:2) NLT.*

CHAPTER SIX

PRIVATE BECOMES PUBLIC

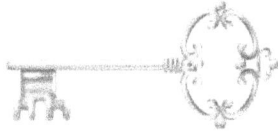

*M*y ex-husband was an expert at Karate; at least I know he was good at the physical feats, however he neglected to apply the discipline of the code of conduct to his life. He had his black belt in the art of karate which based on the response of his peers, was an admirable achievement. Recently, I made note of the Code of Conduct at my grandchildren's karate school, and they are similar to all schools that teach Karate.

- Respect: Should show respect to all people

- Discipline: Dedicate to self-improvement and

  punctuality

- Good judgment: Good judgment in all decisions;

  never make decisions based on selfishness

- Self-control: Control attitude, anger and actions; seek positive ways to dispel anger
- The Golden Rule: Treat others as you yourself would like to be treated

The discipline of Karate teaches self-control and courage. Maybe this was played out in other areas of his life, but it was not evident at home. He was an abusive man and many restraining orders were issued against him, which he ignored and violated. While I was not always living in fear of him for the entire 7 years of our marriage, I became more and more concerned during the last year when his abusive behavior escalated.

I remember this particular period of time when I was walking around in fear. He had violated the restraining order again, but beyond that, his behavior was getting more threatening and intimidating. He would call the house uttering profanities and threatening to shoot me and the rest of my family members.

One day I was on my way to work and scouting my environment as I was then programmed to do, due to my heightened sense of insecurity, I saw him in my rear view mirror. I continued on my way, trying at all cost to evade him. He was so bent on pursuing me that he ended up rear ending me. In essence he became a stalker and I was being stalked. I do not remember the outcome of that particular day, as the numbers of occurrences were such that some of them merge in my mind.

Another episode of dysfunction happened one day when we had a disagreement. What transpired between the time of the argument and the moment he revived me was lost. I was out cold and he revived me with smelling salts. After the incident I was existing in a fog. I wondered what was happening to me, why I would get dizzy and lightheaded, but I never connected the dots that I was hit in the head and had sustained injury. When I went to the doctor, I was informed that I had sustained a punctured eardrum.

That incident opened my eyes to the stark reality that he could have killed me. I was scare. I believe he was scared too. As usual, he was apologetic but this time he had fear in his eyes. I wonder if he was more fearful of what he was capable of doing like murder or manslaughter; or was he scared of what he saw in me. This time my response was definitely different. I was not reacting, in fact, I was not even responding to his efforts at apologies. I was in a "far away experience". I was looking beyond the immediate situation and contemplating my way out.

I was nonverbal, introspective and reflective. I was afraid of the way I was thinking. For the first time in the marriage, I came face to face with the fact that we could not, and would not remain together. What was more frightening was the fact that my mind had gone far beyond the divorce process. I started thinking of ways that I could kill him, before he killed me. I thought about details of the method I would use to kill him, and how I would cover it up. I thank you Lord for rescuing me from myself. The Lord delivered me. That marked the official beginning of the end of us as a couple.

LAST ENCOUNTER

It started out like any other day. I was off from work that day and I got out of bed slowly, just taking things in strides. The day continued in the same pace with no indication that there were "tornadic" activities on the horizon that would cause a complete inside-out shift in my life.

I was on the phone with a friend, when I heard a sound like someone was trying to break into the house. Looking through the window we saw each other. The eyes of my ex-husband looked hard and cold. I knew he was up to no good. The phone went dead as he yanked the cord out of its place and simultaneously, it seemed, the kitchen door opened. He was standing there with an ice-pick in his hand.

Fear gripped my hard like an invisible hand, and I felt the strength in my knees ebbing away. Trying to gather my composure, I was able to timidly ask,

"What are you here for? Are you going to kill me?"

"No! I am not going to kill you; I came to see how you have rearranged the place."

All that rushed through my mind was the many restraining orders that he had violated, how he had expressed that he did not care about the cops, that he was doing "target practice" in Ft. Lauderdale and that someday they would find my body in the garbage dump.

It's amazing how "fear" can block all sense of logics, reasoning, and sense of what is at your disposal. I have studied and learned many scriptures, which are written to sustain you. There I was in dire need and I was a complete blank. In fact, I was so numb that I believe minutes passed which still remain blank until this day.

I was jolted back into reality when he started pushing me towards the bedroom. He was still talking the same foolish talk, "I come to see how you have rearranged the place." The stark reality of my plight sunk in and I was sinking to the ground. At this point my mind started working.

I called out:

"Jesus" My voice was a mere whisper.

"Jesus" I called a second time. It was weak, but louder.

"Jesus" I mustered up all that I had in me and the third time I called Him.

I expected him to back off, thinking that at the Name of Jesus, he would show reverence, seeing that he also was a believer, or was he?

I have heard of the "Shakanah" glory of God and could only imagine what that was like. At the third call of His name, Jesus was in the room with me. He brought with Him, hope and reassurance. I wanted to stay in this experience forever, but it was very short-lived. There was a knock at the door and a brother from the church was calling my name.

My ex husband grabbed me by the throat and put the ice pick to my face, telling me to be quiet. All that came out was a muffled sound.

"Where is the presence of the Lord?" I wondered.

I was so puzzled and distraught.

"Where are you?" I asked God in my mind. "Did you just come to trick me?"

I wondered as the enemy put doubt in my mind. Thank God that our spiritual security is not dependent on our feelings. I was consumed with fear. The strength that I had gotten a few minutes before ebbed away, as I heard the brother from the church leave.

I cried to God inwardly;

"He is gone, he is gone, are you tricking me? Are you leaving me too?"

My God did not hold my doubt against me. The contemplation was short-lived because soon I heard a loud voice on the loudspeaker.

It was the cops.

"You are surrounded", one said over the horn.

"Come out with your hands up!" he kept repeating.

It took hours of contemplating, pleading, and negotiating with me, before the gravity of his situation dawned on him. After a while he started getting agitated, pacing back and forth with his hands on his head. Looking through the windows, he saw about ten cops around the house. Some were in the front, others in the back, and some were on their bellies with guns pointing at the house. The street was full of neighborhood people. It was like a bad movie.

I was held hostage in that house for about two hours. As he pleaded, reasoned, and negotiated with me, I began to feel sorry for him. Even when I was at last free to escape, I remained there. Why? I do not know and it did not make sense. I guess I was struggling with the same disease that many abused wives grapple with, *Battered Wife Syndrome**. (See resource page)

When I finally came to the opened door and the cop said;

"Come out with your hands up". I was so scared, I almost wet my pants. I obeyed and came out with my hands up. I heard someone say,

"No, it's Venoris", and my brother came towards me and hugged me.

I watched them handcuff and carry my ex-husband off to jail. I was taken in the police car to the precinct where they took a statement and pictures. I was shocked to see how my face was swollen and my clothes torn up, with no recollection of why it would have been so severe.

What had transpired on my behalf then was a set-up that God orchestrated. When my ex-husband broke into the house, my friend that I was talking to at the time, kept calling me without getting a response. She realized that I was in trouble and called the police. She had heard when I said that it seemed like someone was trying to break in. Then the phone was yanked out of the wall and she was unable to get me.

I have asked many "Why's". No specific answers have come, but what has satisfied me over the years is the truth of God's many promises. I don't know why we have to go through afflictions to be proven worthy, but I know that He said that His ways are higher than our ways and his thoughts are higher than ours. I accept his word.

"For as the heavens are higher than the earth, so are my ways higher than your ways, and my thoughts than your thoughts" (Isaiah 55:9) KJV.

I take comfort in the fact that He has purpose for my life and He will use whatever means to achieve His purpose.

"Behold, I have refined thee, but not with silver; I have chosen thee in the furnace of affliction" (Isaiah 48:10) KJV.

"As you endure this divine discipline, remember that God is treating you as his own children. Who ever heard of a child who is never disciplined by its father?" (Hebrews 12:7) NLT.

OUT OF THE SHADOWS

After years of living in the shadows the Lord started talking to me about coming out and walking on bright side of the street. On several occasions and by various means, I started sensing that I am supposed to do something about becoming a "victor" and quit being a "victim". I started sensing in my Spirit the call to be an example of one walking in victory instead of defeat; in power instead of weakness and in joyfulness rather than sorrowing. I am an overcomer, and so is every child of God who has been washed in the Blood of Jesus. He has already overcome for us.

"I have told you all this so that you may have peace in me. Here on earth you will have many trials and sorrows. But take heart, because I have overcome the world" (John 16:33) NLT.

Are you living in defeat? Are you living in fear? Has the enemy stripped you of dignity and put a sense of embarrassment and shame upon you because of you past? One of his most successful weapons is secrecy and isolation. He is deceptive and will blame you for even the wrongs that have been perpetrated against you. As you buy into his lies, he succeeds in alienating you, making you feel like you are the only person that things like this happen to, and you end up trying to cover up your misappropriated shame. By this he succeeds in alienating you.

The reality is this: The people, who you are hiding from and are trying to impress, sometimes have greater dark secrets and bigger skeletons in their closets that you could ever dream of. To beat the enemy you cannot negotiate with him or try to coexist peacefully with him. You have to admit where you are, bring it to your heavenly father in prayer and fight the enemy with the weapons that He (God) has given you. Be encouraged because we know Satan's end.

"One day the members of the heavenly court came again to present themselves before the Lord, and the Accuser, Satan, came with them" (Job 2:1) NLT.

"Then I heard a loud voice shouting across the heavens, "It has come at last—salvation and power and the Kingdom of our God, and the authority of his Christ. For the accuser of our brothers and sisters has been thrown down to earth—the one who accuses them before our God day and night" (Rev.12:10)NLT.

"We use God's mighty weapons, not worldly weapons, to knock down the strongholds of human reasoning and to destroy false arguments" (2Corinthians 10: 4.) NLT.

"A final word: Be strong in the Lord and in his mighty power. [11] Put on all of God's armor so that you will be able to stand firm against all strategies of the devil. [12] For we are not fighting against flesh-and-blood enemies, but against evil rulers and authorities of the unseen world, against mighty powers in this dark world, and against evil spirits in the heavenly places. [13] Therefore, put on every piece of God's armor so you will be able to resist the enemy in the time of evil. Then after the battle you will still be standing firm. [14] Stand your ground, putting on the belt of truth and the body armor of God's

righteousness. [15] ***For shoes put on the peace that comes from the Good News so that you will be fully prepared.*** [16] ***In addition to all of these, hold up the shield of faith to stop the fiery arrows of the devil.*** [17] ***Put on salvation as your helmet, and take the sword of the Spirit, which is the word of God" (Ephesians 6:10-17) NLT.***

So you see, the Lord has not left us defenseless. He has provided us with the weapons we need to defeat the enemy. The enemy has stolen much from us but he is going to return all that he has stolen, sevenfold even to a hundredfold. So! Come out from your shadow! Declare who you are in Christ! Resist the enemy and use your weapons! Put on your helmet; put on your breastplate and your loincloth. Pick up your shield and get your sword in your hand. Let us conquer the enemy in Jesus Name.

As I write, a resolute spirit is welling up inside of me and the power of faith is taking a hold of me. It is just awesome to experience the Spirit of the living God working in my life. I can truly say like the psalmist **"It is good for me that I have been afflicted; that I might learn thy statutes" (Psalm 119:71) KJV.**

"For every child of God defeats this evil world and we achieve this victory through our faith" (1 John 5:4).

"No, despite all these things, overwhelming victory is ours through Christ, who loved us" (Romans. 8:37).

I returned to a book I used to read years ago <u>Praying Bible Promises</u> by Clift and Kathleen Richards (Victory House, Inc 1998). A quote from this book:

"The power of faith emanating from the word of God, protected by the blood of Jesus and empowered by the Holy Spirit, fulfills the promises in our lives. Many people seem unaware of these sources of tremendous power that are available to us. It is the promises of God that reveal their power to us".

"But if the Spirit of Him that raised up Jesus from the dead dwell in you, He that raised up Christ from the dead shall also quicken your mortal bodies by His Spirit that dwelleth in you" (Romans8:11).

The Spirit of God is quickening me. The love of God is constraining me from going off and "leaning to my own understanding". I am learning to get into a daily surrender to God; otherwise all that He has for me can become overwhelming, or become a source of pride.

CHAPTER SEVEN

SUN STAND STILL

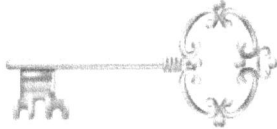

As I hear about other people's experiences of impasse in their lives, and also experience times of perplexing roadblock in my own relationships, I think about a book that I read a little while ago about believing God for the "impossible things in life". It talks about audacious faith. The name of the book is <u>Sun Stand Still</u> by Steven Furtick (Multnomah Books -2010).

The sad thing about all this is the fact that there are great truths within the pages of this book, yet I have forgotten most of what I read. I hasten to reassure myself that it is O.K. anyway, because to get even a morsel at a time is good. As long as we apply a little at a time, it is good. What impacted me most in this book is the challenge to audacious faith; daring to ask God for the impossible and having the faith to believe for it in my life.

I do believe that the same God who worked miracles years ago is the same unchanging God that I serve. He even held up His own work, going contrary to His own natural order of nature on His children's behalf. When God wants to do something remarkable for His children, He will do what it takes to accomplish it, even to suspend nature. This was proven in the lives of several men of old. He stopped the sun for 24 hours on behalf of Joshua (Joshua 10:12-14), Jesus walked on the water (Matt. 14:25), Enoch was translated (Genesis: 5:24), and Elijah also was translated and taken up to heaven without physically dying (2Kings2:11). God did it then and He is still powerful to do it now.

Are those people mentioned different from us? Let's explore further, the unusual experiences of their lives.

JOSHUA

How did the sun stand still? In relation to the earth, the sun is always standing still. It is the earth that revolves around the sun; however the terminology used in Joshua should not cause us to doubt the miracle. After all, we are not confused when someone tells us the sun rises or sets. The real point is that the day was prolonged. Regardless of what explanation used, the Bible is clear that the day was prolonged by a miracle, and that God's intervention turned the tide of the battle for His people.

Characteristics

- Demonstrated his faith in God by taking leadership of Israel, after Moses death

- Demonstrated solidarity in his obedience to God

- Destroyed all the idols. Had faith in God only

- Urged Israel to continue to follow God and Him only

- Submission to God was exemplary. When God spoke, Joshua listened

ENOCH

Not much is said of Enoch, but the Bible states that Enoch lived for 365 years. He had a close relationship with God and when his years were up, he was rewarded my being translated and taken directly to heaven, bypassing death.

ELIJAH

Elijah was one of the two most notable prophets that ministered during the dark period when Israel was ruled by evil kings. His successor was Elisha. Elijah also was rewarded by being translated and taken directly to heaven, bypassing death. Aside from Jesus, Enoch and Elijah were the only two humans to be translated to heaven without dying. Other characteristics of Joshua include:

- Predicted beginning and ending of three-year drought

- Was used by God to restore a dead baby to his mother

- Represented God in a show-down with priests of Baal and Asherath

JESUS

The Bible is replete with documentation of miracles performed by Jesus. He is actually in a different category of men, but is included here because of His own statement that we will do greater works that He did. It's almost unbelievable, but Jesus actually said it. So what is hindering us from doing these great works? It must be that we are not taking up our rightful position of "ruling and taking dominion that Jesus secured for us, by dying on the cross.

"I tell you the truth, anyone who believes in me will do the same works I have done, and even greater works, because I am going to be with the Father" (John 14:12) NLT.

The day did not lengthen for me, nor did I walk on the water, but, I have had some "Sun stand still" experiences in my life when, I know that if God did not intervene on my behalf, I would have been doomed. I believe that the Lord is working in me, stretching my level of faith even as I write. My desire is to get to deeper place of trust in Him. I embrace audacious faith.

Yes! Miracles still happen; one reason why we do not see the hand of God is because of our mind-set. Unfortunately the human mind-set is geared at explaining things away. We always try to find a human or scientific explanation for it. The natural man, influenced by the devil, will always attribute the accolades that belong to God to some other source. However God still works on behalf of His people; and I daresay on behalf of us all. He is merciful.

"For he gives his sunlight to both the evil and the good, and he sends rain on the just and the unjust alike" (Matthew 5:25).

"The rain pours down from the clouds and everyone benefits" (Job 36:28).

Another reason that we do not see God's hand at work operating intentionally on our behalf is due to a lack of commitment on our part. Throughout the scripture, we see where the nation of Israel was charged with Idolatry. Well, we in this present day are guilty of the same thing. We put many things before God. In fact many of us do not honor God at all. We turn to Him when we are in trouble and expect Him to deliver us. We are no different from Idolatrous Israel. When we turn to Him, we pray, fast, read the word, and pray some more, and seem to come around full circle. God's promises are true and He is a covenant-keeping God. He watches over His word to bring them to pass in our lives. However there are conditions to every single promise. He does His part; we are required to do our part. He expects us to be faithful and adhere to the conditions of His word. That is the way that He honors us. That is when we will see His hand at work in our lives.

"Understand, therefore, that the LORD your God is indeed God. He is the faithful God who keeps his covenant for a thousand generations and lavishes his unfailing love on those who love him and obey his commands"(Deuteronomy 7:9)NLT.

Because Jesus came and died for us, taking back what the devil had stolen from us, He has limited His demonstration of power, waiting on believers to do the works that He has designed for us to do. God still works in the natural and the supernatural on behalf of His children, but He has limited His manifestations, as He urges us on to take our rightful place in taking authority in His name. He yearns to teach us; we just need to change our focus to the things of God. We have to know who we are in Christ, and know that He is really the True and Living God.

Not only have I seen the hand of God operational in my life personally, my calling as a Prayer Intercessor allows me the awesome privilege of been a part of people's stories. I share in their sorrows, weeping with them at times and, thank God, able to rejoice with them many times.

I prayed with JB years ago when I was a part of the prayer ministry at Church of God of West Broward. I was on the prayer Line. I would go to the church on

Wednesdays and call up people who were on the "sick and shut in" list and pray with them. At this time the prayer ministry was new, and the prayer line concept had not been popular with the people, so although the prayer line number was in the bulletin, the people were not really calling. In calling and getting these people engaged in prayer, the blessing became two- fold. Many would express how relived they were after the prayer, some were in tears and we would end up rejoicing together. I would wonder who was more blessed, them or me. I had the passion for the ministry.

I did not know JB personally at the time, but after a while, there was a very good connection as I was calling her every week for a while; she was going through a tough season of her life. After a while we lost contact as the issues resolved, or so I thought at the time, as her name did not show up on the list anymore. This was about ten years ago.

Sometime in August 2011 while I was talking with my sister, she mentioned JB's name and said that there was need to pray. My Sister did not know much, but she said that it was health issues. We interceded together on JB's behalf, and I make a mental promissory note to continue to pray. A few days later, JB called me. We prayed together asking God for healing from cancer, and asking for direction and protection for the upcoming surgery which was scheduled for the following week. We prayed with a deep understanding that God hears us and cares for us.

"And if we know that he hear us, whatsoever we ask, we know that we have the petitions that we desired of him" (1 John 5:15) KJV.

At this time, JB was more concerned about her husband, who had always been her rock and now he was devastated with all that was ailing his wife.

JB'S STORY IN HER OWN WORDS

"20 years ago after the birth of my last daughter, I received some news from the physician that changed my whole family. What started out as an awesome period of time quickly changed, when I received the diagnosis of Rheumatoid Arthritis. My life was turned upside down and since then it has been an uphill battle. It has taken a toll on me emotionally, physically, and at times even spiritually. The medications prescribed for the disease, adversely affected me, with almost as much side effect as the disease itself. I kept switching medication so frequently; it was hard to keep up. I could not keep track.

Rheumatoid Arthritis tends to be debilitating in nature, and I have been experiencing that effect. Many times I was consumed with pain, which progressed to the point where simple daily activities, like showering and getting in and out of bed was a major feat. As time went on, I even ended up having surgery, due to the deformity of my hand bones. During this ordeal, I purposed in my heart to continue to praise my way through.

Just when I thought I had a handle on it, I was faced with another obstacle. I started having severe headaches and visual disturbances. After having MRI of the brain, it was discovered that I had sustained a stroke. I lost my peripheral vision. At this time also I was diagnosed with glaucoma which was attributed to side effect of the medications. I was beginning to feel like a medical mystery

Needless to say, I was experiencing the challenge of my life. Depression kept hovering and it took all the effort that I could muster up to stay afloat. I kept holding on the scriptures, especially Ephesians 6: 10-11. I never lost my Hope in God.

"Finally, be strong in the Lord and in his mighty power. Put on the full armor of God, so that you can take your stand against the devil's schemes" (Ephesians 6: 10-11).

Thank God for a loving and supportive family, for friends, and of course, I thank God for who He is in my life. He has been with me through it all. My husband was my "rock", and my daughters were right there along with him. I had down times, when I was mad at myself, mad at everyone around me, and mad at the world. There were many valley episodes, but "thank God", for in the valley "He restoreth my soul". I realize that He kept restoring me.

A most remarkable turnaround came one night. I was in so much pain I laid on the floor and began crying out to God. I told the Lord:

"I can't take the pain anymore. I just want to give up."

I was desperate. As I finally fell asleep I heard a voice say;

"Joy cometh in the morning."

When I woke up, I was feeling better than I had felt in years. From that point on, I have kept claiming my healing. I still have problems but I have confidence in God as He helps me on the journey. I am constantly casting my cares on Him. I now have a new outlook on life.

I recently went to the doctor for a routine visit only to leave with news of abnormal growth cells multiplying in my body. I was battling cancer. The word "cancer" itself sounds like a death sentence. It's a word no one wants to hear. It's like a plague in today's society. I went to God about it, just like I do about everything in my life.

God has been doing a work within me because when my doctor gave me the bad news, I was not as concerned about myself as I was about my family. My husband took the news very badly. He has always been my rock and now here he was in such an uncertain place. It was mind-boggling to see him so broken. I'm sure God had him in mind when He decided to give us the miracle.

We agreed on surgery as the course of action; however God had a set-up for me and my family. The pathology results came back with no evidence of cancer cell. Besides my physical health, God also had a plan to refresh and restore my family. What was meant to break us down actually empowered us to be closer and stronger than ever. Thanks be to God!"

Her favorite verse of scripture:

"Trust in the LORD with all your heart and lean not on your own understanding; in all your ways acknowledge Him and He will direct your path" (Proverbs 3:5) NLT.

So JB is cancer-free. Miracles do happen, but are we acknowledging them? The Sun stood still for her. God intercepted the plan of the enemy who "comes to steal, to kill and to destroy"

"The thief cometh not, but for to steal, and to kill, and to destroy: I am come that they might have life, and that they might have it more abundantly." **(John 10:10) KJV**

PURPOSE OF PRAYER

I came to a heightened awareness of the purpose of prayer and this awareness has added great dimension to my prayer life. I understand that God loves us so much and want us to be partakers of His great work on earth. Because of this, He puts on our hearts what He really wants to accomplish on earth, which already is accomplished in heaven. As we then pray what he has put on our hearts, we are actually praying His will for our situation on earth. We are praying "thy will be done on earth as it is already done in heaven".

In his book, Shadows come to Light (African Christian Press 2000), Dr Samuel Ofori Onwona points out that *"Prayer is the most effective God-given ammunition for accomplishing our destiny here on earth"*. It is our direct line of communication with God. Without it we cannot take our right place of rule and taking dominion in the earth. It is an awesome awareness to grasp the concept that I am actually partnering with God. Praise you Jesus. Thank you for such love.

Let us not take the privilege prayer lightly. Prayer is our direct link to heaven and is how we get to speak to God and for Him to speak to us. In the previous dispensation, before Christ, the people went to God through the human priest. Jesus came and broke down that middle wall that separated us from Him and He gave us free access into the throne room of Glory. No more do we have to go through a human priest to access God, but we go through Jesus, God's son, who the scripture refers to as the Great High Priest. God has made this provision for us and we now have direct communication with Him. If we neglect prayer, then we are cutting our mode of communication with our Father. How would you function in this life without a telephone?

"But now you have been united with Christ Jesus. Once you were far away from God, but now you have been brought near to him through the blood of Christ. For Christ himself has brought peace to us. He united Jews and Gentiles into one people when, in his own body on the cross, he broke down the wall of hostility that

separated us. He did this by ending the system of law with its commandments and regulations. He made peace between Jews and Gentiles by creating in himself one new people from the two groups" (Ephesians 2:13-15) NLT.

"So Christ has now become the High Priest over all the good things that have come. He has entered that greater, more perfect Tabernacle in heaven, which was not made by human hands and is not part of this created world. With his own blood—not the blood of goats and calves— he entered the Most Holy Place once for all time and secured our redemption" (Hebrews 9:11-12) NLT.

"And so, dear brothers and sisters, we can boldly enter heaven's Most Holy Place because of the blood of Jesus. By his death, Jesus opened a new and life-giving way through the curtain into the Most Holy Place. [21] And since we have a great High Priest who rules over God's house, let us go right into the presence of God with sincere hearts fully trusting him. For our guilty consciences have been sprinkled with Christ's blood to make us clean, and our bodies have been washed with pure water." (Hebrews 10:19-22) NLT.

COMMUNICATION

There are difficulties in communication in every relationship, and marriage is no exception. This issue is apparent every day. No doubt this plan of the enemy, Satan, is to cause havoc in the foundational structure of the society; after all, the home is the nucleus of the society. This started from the beginning and continues to this day, where Satan sowed the seed of discord between our forefather Adam and his wife Eve. God came to our aid, sent His son Jesus to die for us and redeemed us back to Himself. With redemption mankind gained back the rule over the enemy so we now can walk in victory. So why are we walking in defeat?

JESUS....WON THE VICTORY

God has done only what God could do. He now requires us to do what we must do to walk in victory. Jesus did not go to the cross to redeem us, for us to walk around passively being whipped by the devil as we cry "Lord help me, Lord help me". No! He has given us authority and we have to war. We have to take back what the enemy has stolen. We have to take back our homes, our spouses and our children who are on drugs. We have to take back our marriages. Take back our cities and our communities. We have to take back our country that is at the brink of disaster. As people of God, we have to be adamant in taking back what the enemy has stolen from us as.

"And from the time John the Baptist began preaching until now, the Kingdom of Heaven has been forcefully advancing, and violent people are attacking it" (Matt.11:12) NLT.

"And from the days of John the Baptist until now the kingdom of heaven suffereth violence, and the violent take it by force" (Matt 11:12) KJV.

"We are human, but we don't wage war as humans do. We use God's mighty weapons, not worldly weapons, to knock down the strongholds of human reasoning and to destroy false arguments. ⁵ We destroy every proud obstacle that keeps people from knowing God. We capture their rebellious thoughts and teach them to obey Christ"

(2Corinthians 10:3-5) NLT.

He has conquered death and the grave for us, left us the Holy Spirit as our "present help in time of trouble", and gave us the weapons to fight with; so what prevents us? Is it laziness, or apathy, or fear of being ostracized, or doubt? What? Whatever it is, it's not worth our souls. We have to fight in order to win! We have heaven on our side as we engage in this warfare of faith. Jesus pointed this out about the enemy we are fighting.

"Or else how can one enter into a strong man's house, and spoil his goods, except he first bind the strong man? And then he will spoil his house" (Matthew 12:29) KJV.

"For when a strong man like Satan is fully armed and guards his palace, his possessions are safe until someone even stronger attacks and overpowers him, strips him of his weapons, and carries off his belongings"

(Luke11:21-22) NLT.

We are in a spiritual warfare. If we do not blind the strongman, then he succeeds in destroying us. We cannot use physical means to annihilate this strongman, but we use the spiritual weapons in the name of Jesus. Jesus instructs us that whatever we do in word or deed, we must do all in His name. Jesus has been victorious for us and is still fighting for us; however we have to be engaged on our own behalf.

"But when people keep on sinning, it shows that they belong to the devil, who has been sinning since the beginning. But the Son of God came to destroy the works of the devil" (1John 3:8) NLT.

132

CHAPTER EIGHT

KEEPING IT ALL IN PERSPECTIVE

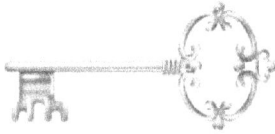

"*Y*our Ministry is birthed out of your deepest pain". I heard this statement years ago and it came back to me yesterday as I met with a couple at their home for lunch. In conversation I remember saying something like this:

"I wish I could really write freely from my heart, without restraints."

"Well, why can't you?" he said.

"Because 'freely and from my heart' would mean opening a part of my heart that involves my husband, and that's not fair to him." I responded.

"What's unfair about it?"

"It's his life too and he is very private." was my response.

As we went back and forth with this dialogue, we finally got to a point where my answer unveiled the whole truth of the matter. You see, my initial answer did not convey the whole truth, but partial truth. The reasons for lack of transparency were twofold.

- Fear

- Concern about privacy issues for my husband.

Fear is a powerful weapon of the enemy. It can inactivate and cripple those who are in its clutches. It intimidates and isolates and causes one to hide away. In this position, confidence ebbs away and that person is alone with no desire to express herself/himself, to share or to seek help. When the challenges of life face this person, he/she gets lost and faint by the wayside, if no-one steps in to help. I am now very acutely aware that the enemy takes a grip and establishes a stronghold in areas where people are isolated and vulnerable.

In the areas where there are embarrassing secrets, where people are hiding with a sense of shame, and where there is fear of exposure, the enemy prevails. God sent His son that we might have abundant life. Abundant living does not include fear. The people of God are called upon to be bold and courageous, even in the midst of our uncertain and messed-up situations. Boldness is not recklessness impulsiveness, but courage to press on through our fears to do what we know is right.

The answer to this dilemma of hiding away in fear is in God.

"So you have not received a spirit that makes you fearful slaves. Instead, you received God's Spirit when he adopted you as his own children. Now we call him, "Abba, Father" (Romans 8:15) NLT.

"For God has not given us a spirit of fear and timidity, but of power, love, and self-discipline" (2 Timothy 1:7) NLT.

Before I left the house, the three of us had an impassioned session of prayer, pouring it all out to our Lord to remove all hindrances and barriers and to release us to do what we've been called to do. In that prayer, I remember being consciously aware of praying about my ministry being birthed of my deepest pain and I asked the Lord to show me and lead me.

I believe that the Lord deals with all His children uniquely. That is why I highly respect people's conviction, and I would never beat down their faith. I am opened to discuss issues of faith, to a certain point; and I welcome people who try to guide, encourage, and teach me concerning the things of God. But when it comes to a deep conviction where God is saying something definitive on an issue, I treat that with utter respect.

I find that the Lord does not just get to the point with me. He mostly strings me along a long journey for a long time. On this journey, I have to dig deep for the hidden treasures. Sometimes I wonder if they are even there. I wonder at times, if I am more stubborn or difficult than anybody else to have to endure so long before I see any result; and then, when the results come, they are like mercy drops only. I know that I sound ungrateful, but I am just being very frank. I ask the Lord to forgive me if I am being ungrateful. When I see others getting ready answers, I question God.

I am glad that the Lord allows me to be real with Him, and He does not condemn me. I am aware that as the Lord deals with us in His unique way for us, I cannot compare myself to others. My Lord has required of me not to take the easy way out. He said that I should be patient and endure. This statement has kept me peeled to the script of my life, when almost everyone rolls their eyes. I say "The love of God constrains me to dig deeper for the meaning of my life."

STANDING GROUND

Another reason why I stand my ground, when all indication says otherwise, is because I get so energized when I see the hand of God making the difference in my life, as opposed to me handling it myself. I serve an all-powerful, ever-present, all-wise God who has set conditions under which his children should function. He wants us to prove Him and to honor His word. The principles of Scripture tell me enough to know that I do not quit, unless He says so. For me, my life is not just finding the easy way out. God is after my spiritual character rather than my comfort. I have to take up my cross and follow Him.

"Then calling the crowd to join his disciples, he said, "If any of you wants to be my follower, you must turn from your selfish ways, take up your cross, and follow Me" (Mark 8:34) NLT.

"I have told you all this so that you may have peace in me. Here on earth you will have many trials and sorrows. But take heart, because I have overcome the world." (John 16:33)NLT.

The crosses we are called to carry are very different, but no cross is light and pleasant to carry. It cuts against everything that the natural mind desires. Our cross propels us from the norm and the mundane to the realm of the Spirit where the Holy Spirit waits to deepen our faith, increase our power, cement our peace and strengthen our courage to keep going the extra mile. I have great expectation of God and at this stage of my life I am very, very expectant. So I stand and I wait to see how He will work.

I woke up to a new day with my Soul crying out this Prayer:

Lord, make me an instrument of your peace

Where there is hatred, let me sow Love

Where there is injury, Pardon

Where there is doubt, Faith

Where there is despair, Hope

Where there is darkness, Light

Where there is sadness, Joy

Oh! Devine Master

Grant; That I may not so much seek

To be consoled, as to console

To be understood, as to understand

To be loved, as to love

For it is in giving that we receive

It is in pardoning, that we are pardoned

It is in dying, that we are born to eternal Life

I greatly desire to be an instrument of His peace.

PURPOSE

My purpose for writing is to publish my autobiography, with awareness that expressing the hidden things of the heart, releases the writer and serves as a source of encouragement and release for others. I towed with the idea then, of writing an inspirational book, instead of an autobiography, since I am still learning to embrace this new concept of openness. At this point, my primary reason for hesitancy is exposing the private parts of my life that affects my husband. I do respect his privacy. I am fully aware though that the Lord is calling me to let my life encourage and release others, so I am writing my story. I remember yesterday's prayer "pulling down barriers and asking to be unhindered as I write" so I bring it again before the Lord.

If we are honest we can all agree that relationships are very difficult all across the board. How can two imperfect human beings be put together with the purpose of finding perfection? It cannot happen. In this life we will have conflicts. The issue is how do we handle conflicts? The relationships that survive are the ones that work wisely at implementing coping tools to handle conflicts. The ones that do not make it do not know how; and maybe do not want to know how, but want to selfishly continue on the easy path; because at the root of the dysfunction in relationship is selfishness.

Successful marriages take on a mindset of endurance, courage and strength beyond the ordinary. If it was an easy thing that naturally fall into place, the divorce rate would not be so high. If it was a thing that money, or fame, or pretty looks could fix, Hollywood would be the forerunner in marriage bliss.

Having been married before, and now married again (previous marriage having failed), I can testify to the fact that the source of the problem can arise from some very unfamiliar and unexpected places. The source of the problem is not always about the other person either; quite often the source of the problem comes from our own blind spots. One person cannot always be right and the other always wrong. Like Shakespeare said "It's not in our stars, but in ourselves that we are underlings." Sometimes we are the underlings.

With all that said, what's the answer? In looking for fulfillment in life, we try various means including marriage. We find out that it is not all that we thought it would be, so we want "out". We look around and alas, here comes someone else looking more promising, so we try to pursue this new opportunity, only to be let down again. It is safe to ask "What is this all about?" Unfortunately this is all about the futility of chasing after the mirage that present itself before us in this present life. Paul said;

"Not that I was ever in need, for I have learned how to be content with whatever I have" (Philippians 4:11) NLT.

"Everything is wearisome beyond description. No matter how much we see, we are never satisfied. No matter how much we hear, we are not content" (Ecclesiastes1:8) NLT.

An attitude of discontentment will cause us to be always looking for what seems better. Paul expressed in Phil. 4:11

that he has learned in whatever state he finds himself to be content. Does it mean that it is wrong to aspire to a better place, or to have better in life? "No!" It means that we should not deceive ourselves into thinking that the "grass is greener on the other side"; rather we should work at problem-solving. Solomon, in Ecclesiastes 1:8 confirms that basically, human beings are dissatisfied.

Living a life of ease and quick fix in relationships brings instant but temporary gratification. Some people choose this way, rather than working out issues and trying to grow in grace. I have heard some thoughts about why people stay in tough relationships:

- Weak (Lack courage)

- A cop-out from really pursuing life

- Fear

From my experience maybe a combination of these factors are influencing my life; however the prevailing factor that drives my decision in my relationship is to see the hand of God move in a mighty way in my life. Jesus challenged his disciples then and is speaking to us now about surrendering our lives to Him. I know that God is able and that He desires for me to trust Him, rather than to take the easy way out.

"Then, calling the crowd to join his disciples, he said, "If any of you wants to be my follower, you must turn from your selfish ways, take up your cross, and follow me" (Mark 8:34) NLT.

To live a committed and surrendered life to Christ calls for great sacrifice and great patience. Without a shadow of a doubt, I know that there is a spiritual purpose for all incidents in my life, whether good or bad. Until the purpose is achieved I stay in my place, until the Lord, who deals with us uniquely, says otherwise. I know that this concept of long suffering and enduring is not an easy pill for us to swallow because mostly we believe that our purpose in this life is to enjoy it to the best we can. I am sorry to be the "party-pooper" and put a damper on your view. I am sure you will agree that when all is said and done, the quick-fix always leave you dissatisfied, disillusioned and still searching. Living for God has promise.

"If you cling to your life, you will lose it; but if you give up your life for me, you will find it" (Matthew10:39) NLT.

THE PIE

At 3:00 clock in the morning, I am musing over the picture of "A Pie" that the Lord showed me about six months ago. I was praying about relationships in general, for my children's lives, and specifically for my own relationship at home with my husband. The Lord showed me a pie, sliced up in various dimensions, with each part representing a different part of my life. He pointed out to me that my marriage is only a very small part of the pie, and cautioned me not to let any part of my life consume or overtake the whole pie.

This most valuable lesson comes back to me as I try, not just to look at my life in the proper perspective, but to write with the passion to encourage others. Is this not just like our God? He gives visual aids to help my memory. He knows that I like pictures and He has a way of taking care of our little fetishes, plus He has a sense of humor.

Although my marriage is only a small part of the "pie" of my life, it is very important part to me; again it is not my whole life. The Lord was gracious to me in showing me how to take it all in perspective. This has helped me to weather the storms of life. I amplify the areas that are working well and downplay what is faulty. Granted, sometimes the bad seems to outweigh the good, but in my experience, eventually the scale tilts the other way and a balance is created.

The issues of my life have helped me to deal with my tendency to be impatient. As I get older, I am realizing that many of the things that I used to agitate about do not even matter. What matters now is that I am learning a different level of patience. The sooner I learn it, the better off I will be. I might even get to a place where I have fewer problems. I say this with a sense of humor because of what the scripture says about impatience. In the scriptures, patience and tribulation go hand in hand.

"But we glory in tribulations also: knowing that tribulation worketh patience; and patience, experience; and experience, hope: And hope maketh not ashamed" *(Romans 5:3-5) KJV.*

The Lord has given my husband the gift of "Helps". He thrives on helping people, so much so that he will give his last dollar. I have cautioned him about "selling his birthright" on a few occasions. This generous spirit is one of the things that was so attractive to me when we met. This attitude is very refreshing in the selfish world we live in. Do not get the wrong impression that I was a gold-digger looking for someone to take over my bills or anything like that, because I was doing fine on my own. It was just refreshing to see a kind man.

The issue that quickly developed after we got married was disagreement in spending. Acknowledging the fact that God has given him this gift and a ministry of helps, how do we strike a happy medium? Any good thing can become a source of discontent if wisdom is not applied. It remains a source of concern as we work on being uniquely who God has called us to be. It takes wisdom to effectively achieve any good work. Without it chaos is created. My husband truly desires to help everybody. The reality is; we will always have the poor with us in life. Does that mean that we ignore them? NO! We do not neglect them, but we use wisdom in our dealings so that we do not become poor ourselves. I have seen many people take advantage of my husband kindness. Many have pretended that they had no other way out, and they came to him. He likes to be needed. The Lord says we all need wisdom and if we are lacking, we must ask of Him. So I ask for wisdom to know how to deal with people.

"You will always have the poor among you" (*Matthew 26:11*) *NLT.*

"If you need wisdom, ask our generous God, and he will give it to you. He will not rebuke you for asking" (*James 1:5*) *NLT.*

So! Life is just plain difficult, but God's plan is forever true. You may say "If God is so good, why does He allow us to go through such hardships, when He could make it so much easier?" Remember that His ways are beyond our ways.

"My thoughts are nothing like your thoughts," says the LORD. *"And my ways are far beyond anything you could imagine.*

For just as the heavens are higher than the earth, so my ways are higher than your ways and my thoughts higher than your thoughts." (Isaiah 55:8-9)NLT.

GOD'S PLAN

Let us take a look at God's original plan, how we have fallen from it, and His plan for redemption. God planned for us to rule and take dominion over the earth.

"Then God said, "Let us make human beings in our image, to be like us. They will reign over the fish in the sea, the birds in the sky, the livestock, all the wild animals on the earth, and the small animals that scurry along the ground" (Genesis 1: 2)NLT.

Then God set certain guidelines that needed to be adhered to; guidelines such as we have today. Adam and his wife, beguiled by the enemy who had been kicked out of heaven with his co-deceivers, messed up. They sinned by disobeying God and obeying the enemy. Now fallen from grace Adam and Eve forfeited their position to rule and Satan took dominion. The effects of sin, disobedience to God, is seen and felt in our world everyday. Satan rules over people by the power of sin in our lives. So, our forefather had a choice and chose wrongly. You have a choice today. How will you choose?

Again, when you ask the question "If God is so good, why does He allow us to suffer so much", or "Why does a good God allow evil?" Remember that it is because of Adam's choice then, and our choice today that we suffer.

So God had a perfect plan, gave man a choice and man messed up. God in His mercy chose to redeem us to Himself through the second Adam, Jesus Christ. In essence Jesus bought us back by shedding His Blood on the cross. When Adam, our forefather fell, we fell with him. God implemented His contingency plan to redeem mankind to Himself. God sent a notice to Satan:

"And I will cause hostility between you and the woman, and between your offspring and her offspring. He will strike your head, and you will strike his heel."

(Genesis 3:15).

In this verse God was heralding the birth of Jesus, our redeemer. This was already known before the foundation of the world. Jesus being described as the Lamb of God who was slain before the foundation of the world.

"And all that dwell upon the earth shall worship him, whose names are not written in the book of life of the Lamb slain from the foundation of the world" (Rev.13:8). ***Those*** whose names are not written in the Book with be worshipping Satan.

Through Christ, we have hope in God. Jesus came, lived, died, buried and rose again from the dead. When He was crucified, innocent blood was shed to the demise of Satan's plan and rule. Man was then reconciled to God, returning to our rightful position of ruling and taking dominion over the earth.

FORMATIVE YEARS

The single most important question anyone could answer is "What will you do with Jesus?" We will all have to answer this most important question one day. The refrain from a song goes like this:

"What will you do with Jesus?

Neutral you cannot be.

One day your soul will be asking

What will He do with you?"

Growing up, I was a conformist. I toed the line mostly, because I was afraid of spanking at that time. Later in life, I conformed because I did not like confrontations and preferred to keep things in the "status quo". I played it safe, you may say boring! Yes pretty boring. I didn't get into much stuff, didn't experiment with much; I think that I told a few lies here and there when I got into trouble; afterwards I had to repent as my conscience would tear me up. We had this phrase that we would repeat to God when we did wrong "Father forgive me, pardon my sinful soul and body". I find it so hilarious now, because we would just rattle this prayer off without even thinking about the wrong. I had an over acute conscience. I realize now that this is not necessarily good, unless you have a clear concept of truth as portrayed in the word of God. The enemy can sell you a lie and cause you to feel falsely condemned. I thank you Lord for delivering me.

The issues of our teenage life 57 years ago pale, in comparison to the ones affecting our children and young people. The things our grandparents and great grandparents found as "criminal" were "little pranks in today's world, and they were definitely not ignored; in fact they were punished swiftly. As children, we use to get into some very "dumb" stuff. I wonder if we were foolish, bored or just plain dumb.

ANECDOTES

One day I went into the pineapple field to smoke. My father was a chain-smoker and I thought that it would be a good thing to do some adult "stuff". I rolled up dried leaves within newspaper and made a cigarette. I lit it up and took a puff. It went immediately to my head and my stomach and I started getting dizzy. I almost died in the field by myself. Needless to say, that cured me once and for all from smoking. I never ever had the desire since then. I thank you Jesus for delivering this fool. I guess He does take care of fools and babies.

I'll share another anecdote with you.

My father was an excellent cultivator, Mom a home maker. She would also plant little flower beds and vegetable garden around the house, and in the back. They raised animals; goats, cows, donkeys, dogs and such. We even had chickens. I loved the little baby chickens, in fact I was very fascinated by them, just like I am with seeing the mother duck walking around with all the ducklings in a row.

One day Mom went to the market and came back home to find all the baby chickens, 12 in total, dead. No one was taking ownership and to this day, I still cannot conceive of any of us kids doing an awful thing like killing the chickens. It was a sad day, and it has remained a mystery; what happened to the chickens.

From time to time, there were different suggestions about what could have happened. Years afterwards, I started hearing names being called in relation to the death of the 12 chickens. My name was included. Now this was years later when I was in nursing school, the incident had happened about 7 to 10 years earlier. What is very amusing about this is that the person who keeps bringing up this incident to me, and dare to accuse me about it, is my sister Sharon, who is actually 14 years my junior. She is the last of 10 siblings. The nerve of her! Where was she at that time anyway? Maybe she was not even born yet. But my sister is like this; she catches a story, it appeals to her and she runs with it. I love my sister dearly so I embrace all her idiosyncrasies.

I used to get into fights with my siblings for petty things. I am sure that they were very real to us then. I grew up in a large household; Father, Mother and ten children. I refer to those days as the "Dark Ages"; however I do believe I am the better for it today.

Because of my humble beginnings and my spiritual foundation, I have narrowly escaped many of the self-inflicted hardships that many of my counterparts endured and are enduring today. Learning to comply and being obedient paid off. At that time, I did not see real value in my "growing-up" years, but even what seemed as insignificant is turning around to be of great importance today. I place great value on my family and how I was brought up. God has been weaving significance in my journey, even though I was not always aware of Him. He has a plan and a purpose for you and me.

"For God saved us and called us to live a holy life. He did this, not because we deserved it, but because that was his plan from before the beginning of time—to show us his grace through Christ Jesus" (2Timothy1:9) NLT.

"And this is God's plan: Both Gentiles and Jews who believe the Good News share equally in the riches inherited by God's children.

Both are part of the same body, and both enjoy the promise of blessings because they belong to Christ Jesus. By God's grace and mighty power, I have been given the privilege of serving him by spreading this Good News" *(Ephesians 3: 6-7) NLT.*

"God's purpose in all this was to use the church to display his wisdom in its rich variety to all the unseen rulers and authorities in the heavenly places. [11] This was his eternal plan, which he carried out through Christ Jesus our Lord" *(Ephesians 3:10-11) NLT.*

CONFORMING

You do not have to be labeled as a "compliant" person to comply or conform. There are conditions in life that we all have to comply with i.e. on the job, when we travel, with the homeowners association, sports guidelines and other regulations. Why do we struggle so much with compliance with God's laws. The most important guidelines for our lives, we disregard. Why do we find it so difficult to comply, and in fact many choose to ignore them?

We have to deal with God sooner or later. Some people have made a conscious decision to reject God, others have decided not to deal with Him; they choose to stay neutral, and there are those like myself who make a decision to accept Him as personal savior and Lord. I choose to serve Him. We are all held accountable for the decision we make; to decide against, means eternal death, separation from God; accepting Him means eternal life or living with God forever.

Jesus, who died for our sins, has risen and is seated on the right hand of God constantly making intercessions (praying) for us. We have to acknowledge what He has done to be saved.

"Wherefore God also hath highly exalted him, and given him a name which is above every name: That at the name of Jesus every knee should bow, of things in heaven, and things in earth, and things under the earth; And that every tongue should confess that Jesus Christ is Lord, to the glory of God the Father"

(Philippians 2:9-11) KJV

"And be not conformed to this world: but be ye transformed by the renewing of your mind, that ye may prove what is that good, and acceptable, and perfect, will of God" (Romans 12:2) KJV.

We have to be conformed to his will to be at peace with Him.

CHAPTER NINE

UNIQUELY YOU

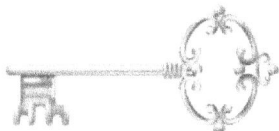

A pivotal point in my life was my experience with Pastor Dr. Owen Facey and the people I interacted with during a course I participated in called "Uniquely You". This was many years ago when I did not even know that God gave His children gifts to function with, and passion to operate those gifts in ministry. This in essence was what the course was about. Before that time, I would "fit in" wherever I went and make the best of it. Sometimes, I have felt like a square peg in a round hole; a real misfit. Since then, I have been released and have found out my real purpose and calling in life. I now function in the area of my giftedness and I am thriving in my spiritual walk. God has not called us all to function the same way. We are unique and He deals with us uniquely. You too can seek and find your unique place in life.

I am sure you will agree that in our society, we are programmed to be what "the societal power that be" says we should be. From elementary school all the way to post graduate institutions, the main aim is to teach us to fit into a script that was pre-programmed, to get some desired outcomes. I understand that we have to follow guidelines, laws, and rules to maintain order. I know that without rules, there would be anarchy. My concern is that there isn't much allowance made for people to explore their unique gifts and talents. Even the church in general has come up short in this area.

There is a place for logics, calculus, and science; but is there a place where people are encouraged to explore their uniqueness? It definitely is not in the established organizations and structures that we see around us. Is there any wonder then that I gravitated to this opportunity to learn and appreciate that I am a unique individual, designed for unique purpose? Since that experience, I have looked at my life in a different way.

I grew up shy and easily intimidated by authority figures. I would easily conform to what was required. In my teenage years, I would push the bar a little, but lacked courage to really explore beyond the limited boundaries of the "Norm". I have kept many thoughts and concerns buried. I was usually the last one to raise a hand in class to ask a question, or contribute to the discussion, especially in large groups. After a while, I realized that there were some unique qualities in me, because the few times when I would speak up and share, the whole interaction would take on a new "slant. It would go to a new direction, but unfortunately not necessarily a better one. Sometimes it became controversial. This was still a good thing because I became aware that my probing thoughts and expressions would provoke certain responses in people. Then I understood that the influence that God had put in me was to be used for His service.

Many thoughts I had, were deep and probing, and many times even controversial. I did not like being controversial, so I would keep my feelings to myself. In the settings where I felt comfortable to speak, I would go into deep probing areas and end up even getting labeled. I remember my cousin labeling me as an "Opposer" when I was a teenager. I now believe that the issue was not with them, but with me. I was not handling the quality God had put in me in the best manner. I did not understand how to channel this unique quality for a better good. Now with the leverage I have gained along my Christian walk and the insight gained during that breakthrough experience in the

"Uniquely You" course, I am able to see life from a different perspective.

I'll give further insight into what the "Uniquely You" course was about. It involved a series of questionnaire, about 70 to 80 questions. In completing these questions, the scores were totaled and reflected in areas of gifts like teaching, preaching, shepherding, helps, etc. The highest scored areas were the areas of giftedness. Another set of exercise was done afterwards that showed where one's passion was. Both went hand in hand mostly. In my case my areas of giftedness were in Encouragement and Intercession primarily; Helps and Teaching (Shepherding) secondarily. Later on, I realized that my passion lined up almost perfectly.

After doing that "Uniquely you" course, I realized that the unique gift that God has given to me, and to all of us, may not be well received. However when channeled in the right way, our gifts become the source of fulfillment and purpose as we take our place in society. We are not here for arbitrary existence, but for purposeful living.

MY MINISTRY

I mentioned before that the Lord showed me that my ministry is birthed out of my deepest pain. As reflected in my writing you can see that there has been enough pain already. I am not sharing as if I am the only one out there experiencing pain, or like mine is the worse. There are millions of people hurting everyday. God is now giving me the boldness to share my story. This will hopefully motivate others to release theirs also. It may not be in the same format of writing a book; it could simply be to share your testimony or your story with the most unlikely person, as the opportunity arises.

I sense that my mission is to encourage. This encouragement is primarily to women who are going through internal struggles of varying sources. Even as I write, I am remembering a patient (was years ago) who was going through deep emotional pain. She had been admitted for some heart problem, but all of a sudden her emotional issues evidenced. She called me into her room and asked me to shut the door behind me. All of a sudden she was weeping uncontrollably; I was at a loss. It was so unexpected. I allowed her to sob, and sob. She was about 60 yrs old. When she was done she said to me:

"This happened to me years ago and you are the first person I am able to tell." She proceeded to tell me about the molestation she had gone through at the hands of her father.

I believe that I have been called and prepared to come alongside people on a one to one basis. I do not desire a platform; I do not need all that to do the simple work God has called me to do. There are enough hurting people around. We see them everyday. If we would have a mindset to reach out and encourage someone as we go along life's way, then we would see a big dent in the vicious cycle of decline that we see around us today.

We have been served notice, "Washington is broken". The government cannot solve the problems. We have been let down over and over as we depended on the physicians to heal us. They continue to try to practice medicine. There are only the few of them who would admit that they do not know. The banks and financial institutions have been bailed out at our expense, and they continue to pocket the profits. The Insurance that we pay into for years, when we need them most they find some clause to deny our coverage. So we end up possibly broke, busted and disgusted; but there is Hope. Always there is Hope in the way God has planned for our lives. We have to reach out neighbor helping neighbor. *"Where is your brother Abel?"(Genesis. 4:9)*

SEEING THE VISION

"Where there is no Vision, the people perish" Proverbs 29:18 (KJV).

One has to come to a settled place to see the Vision. Just like the troubled surface of a lake cannot reflect an image, the fast pace of life will not allow you to see the deep things of God. Do I know it all? No! I admit that I am just learning.

I see a deep purpose in being "put aside" from the usual routine of my life. When I was diagnosed cancer, and experienced that new and unwelcome experience in my life, the Lord showed me that my life is much bigger than cancer or any sickness, bigger that my husband or children, and even bigger than what I do in the church. All parts are significant, but it's only a part of a bigger picture. That helped me to take it all in perspective. All these experiences are being used for a higher good. I now realize that it is good that I have been through it. I came to a slower and reflective place, where I was able to see more clearly.

"Where there is no Vision, the people perish" (Proverbs 29:18) KJV.

I have always looked at this scripture in one light. I used to see this as something in the line of a vision statement, or a plan of action. Lately I am seeing a different aspect. I am seeing vision in an expanded way. The fact that the Lord is sensitizing me to a more purposeful walk is clarifying the vision for me. When I am acutely aware of Him directing me; that's vision for me. When I read the scripture and new meaning jumps out at me; that's vision for me. When I am aware of His presence, and see how He works out something in my favor; that's vision for me. I realize that I was perishing without the clear directive for my life. As I glean deeper understanding I am experiencing new buoyancy in my life. Steven Furtick, in his book

Sun Stand Still, shed some light unto my understanding of the vision for my life. He said;

"If the dream in your heart isn't biblically based, focused on Jesus, affirmed by the key people in your life, and tethered to your passions, gifts, and life experiences, chances are, you are way off prompt."

Furtick points out that everyone is positioned uniquely to fulfill a particular purpose in life, and that discovering and fulfilling that purpose is our calling in life. No one can simply tell us our purpose, it has to be discovered. Simply telling us our purpose, would be cheating us out of the opportunity of discovering who Chris is. He said:

"Discovering God's vision for your life is one of the primary ways God teaches you about His character. Seizing His big purpose for your life is not just about figuring out what God wants from you and getting down to business. It's also about getting intimately acquainted with who Jesus is. It's about mining the depths of who you are in Him. And out of that revelation, you will fulfill the purpose that He put you on earth to fulfill."

I take great pleasure in listening to people's testimonies because I enjoy knowing what God is doing in their lives and among us. I believe Graceann came to that place of clarity in the vision that God has for her life too. Let me share a little of her story with you.

GRACEANN'S STORY

Graceann and I go to the same church and one evening as we walked in together for a concert, we started talking about what the Lord was doing in our lives. I realized then that she had been having an awesome experience as God was turning the table in her favor. She had had many sun stand still moments and she had a great testimony. Be aware that we all have testimonies of God's grace in our lives. We need to sensitive to them. Because of the essence of Graceann's story and the degree of her passion, I felt compelled to ask for her story to be included in my book. She graciously agreed.

Graceann was a shy girl growing up. She became a school teacher and worked in that capacity for two year when; then was a drastic change in her life. She had been trusting the Lord since she accepted Him as Lord and Savior when she was 18 years old.

One day she was on the way to the doctor with her children, when she got the terrible news. Her sister had suddenly died. Her world fell apart. Having to continue on to the doctor, since her kids were kept out of school to be checked out by a cardiologist, she braced herself. At the doctor's office, her husband went in with the children while she cried and cried, asking the Lord why? She had no inhibition as she expressed her concern about whether or not her sister was with the Lord. Graceann said that during this time of utter bewilderment a stranger in the doctor's office walked up to her and said;

"Do not worry; your sister is with the Lord." It was said with such conviction, that she knew it was true.

What gave her further reassurance afterwards was the fact that her sister had sent an e-mail of Psalm 55:22 to all her siblings the night before her death.

"Give your burdens to the LORD, and he will take care of you. He will not permit the godly to slip and fall" **(Psalm 55:22)** *NLT.*

The death of Graceann's sister challenged her faith severely. She said "I still feared God, but not in a reverent way." She was actually afraid of God. Things were not making much sense for Graceann and the reality of her sister's death was staring her and everyone else in the face.

"So what did you do"? I asked her

"God gave me the strength to pull it together and address the real issues. He gave me a burden on my heart for all my family members who were not saved and the courage to speak a most challenging message at the funeral. At the end, 27 family members and friends gave their hearts to the Lord. It was a miracle" she said. She continued to explain that she had no inhibition whatsoever and that the shy Graceann stood up.

We have to agree that God moves in mysterious ways. This was one of those mysterious ways.

Graceann said that after her sister's death she struggled with many issues. Suddenly, she was hospitalized with symptoms that baffled the doctors. During this time she lost her teaching job. This added to her stress and she deteriorated quite rapidly. After ruling out differential diagnoses the doctors determined that she had Idiopathic thrombocytopenic purpura (ITP). All this was happening on the heels of the death of her sister that devastated her entire family. I had an interview with Graceann over lunch.

Venoris: "What exactly is ITP"?

Graceann: "ITP is *a* blood disorder called Idiopathic thrombocytopenic purpura. It is also called Immune Thrombocytopenia Purpura because it is a blood disorder of the immune system. Basically, the Idiopathic part of ITP means in short; "of unknown origin." There is no known cause for ITP and it is more common in children than in adults. Children tend to grow out of it, so in this case it's called acute. Adults with ITP are usually referred to as chronic because it does not go away".

Venoris: "How have you been coping with this illness along with the other issues at home? I know your husband had a heart attack sometime after your illness started"?

Graceann: "Yes, it has been very challenging. It's all about God's grace. There is nothing I can say that I did of myself to get through this. I was a complete mess for a while. I started suffering with anxiety and panic attacks. I feared God, but not in a reverent way. I feared Him as one who wanted to hurt me and not love me. I broke down in complete emotional, mental, and physical exhaustion. Little did I know though that my God was setting me up for another level of my journey.

During my turmoil, it happened that I visited a church where a pastor who I had known, but had not seen for a long time was preaching. At the end of the message he called me out and said to me;

"Daughter of Zion, will you trust me again?"

"Right away, I knew it was from the Lord. This pastor knew nothing about my present struggles. I saw that as a direct call from God..." Graceann said and continued to explain.

"It marked a point of real turn around from that period of my life. Little by little God began drawing me closer and closer to Him. That's not to say that I don't have moments when I feel anxious or fearful, but I have built a spiritual support system around me".

Venoris: "I hear that you have started a ministry for those suffering with chronic illness; tell me about the ministry."

Graceann: "Well, it was during a conference that my husband and I attended that God placed in my heart the need to start a ministry that would serve as a support system for others who were struggling with similar chronic illnesses. Together we started seeking the Lord and brainstorming for names. That night we were given the name L.A.C.I. which stands for Living Above Chronic Illness."

L.A.C.I. is based on **3 John verse 1:2 "Dear friend, I hope all is well with you and that you are as healthy in body as you are strong in spirit"** NLT.

There is also a book entitled L.A.C.I. that further amplifies the purpose of the ministry. It can be purchased through. www.trueperspectivepublishinghouse.com.

Through Graceann's unique journey, she has come to a place of satisfying purpose for her life. Through her experience she now has the Vision, Passion and Determination to affect others who are, or will be experiencing what she already went through.

THOUGH THE OUTER MAN PERISHES

"We never give up. Though our bodies are dying, our spirits are being renewed every day" (2 Corinthians 4:16) NLT.

There is no doubt that the physical body is dying daily, and will eventually die permanently. This is a hard "pill to swallow". The encouraging word is that our spiritual person lives on; either in heaven or hell. We have a choice in where we will live for eternity. We tend to shy away from this, but is a stark reality that we have to face, and sooner rather that later is better. It is an inevitable decision to make.

Everyday we see and hear it on the talk shows and the soap operas, cosmetic procedures that are geared to rebuild and add esthetics to our bodies. Realistically, we cannot fault someone for wanting to improve the appearance or their longevity. We also hear about the pills to help to loose weight, the anti-aging creams, and a whole list of products designed to keep us young. The reality is that the outer man is perishing. The things that we put on are just masks that hide the real truth.

The sad thing is that some people are so vain that they go through the whole list of additives, even at the risk of their health, just to show an appealing face or a fake voluptuous body. Sometime ago this lady was being interviewed on a talk show. She had gone through 20 cosmetic procedures and was still discontented with her looks. At that time she was blaming the doctors, who she claimed, did not steer her in the right direction. Her before and after pictures were displayed. She was a beauty before, and she had very questionable features in the end product. Obviously this woman had deeper issues that cosmetic procedures could not cure.

Although she was an exceptional case, we are all faced with the same dilemma of trying hard to improve our outer bodies, and so we should; However, we aught to come to face to face with the reality that the outer bodies will decline. The word of God tells us that "the outer man will perish". It behooves us then to spent time of building up the inner man that will live forever i.e. the Spirit.

What has shocked me recently is the extent to which we have deteriorated morally. Now the targeted age group has not only gone from adults to teens, but now the children, especially girls, are on the radar. They are falling victim to societal pressures and the marketing companies. They are displaying children's walking shoes that "tightens the legs and lifts the butts", swim suits with padded built in bra to enhance sexiness, to name a few.

Aside from getting caught in the vanities of life, our priorities have completely shifted from spiritual values to strictly satisfying the appetites and the bodies, i.e. sexual, greed, and pleasure. The motto now is "if it looks good, tastes good, feels good, smells good, or even sounds good, then let's go for it". How sad? Remember the wisest man, Solomon, saying "it is all vanity." It is like a vapor; it will disappear.

"Then I looked on all the works that my hands had wrought, and on the labor that I had labored to do: and, behold, all was vanity and vexation of spirit, and there was no profit under the sun". (Ecclesiastes.2:11). KJ.

Solomon laid out the purpose of man i.e. human beings.

"Let us hear the conclusion of the whole matter: Fear God, and keep his commandments: for this is the whole duty of man" (Ecclesiastes 12:13) KJV.

"For God shall bring every work into judgment, with every secret thing, whether it be good, or whether it be" (Ecclesiastes 12:14) KJV.

I will leave you with a final word from Joyce Meyer's devotional

"Ending Your Day Right" (Warner Faith 2004).

COOPERATE WITH GOD'S PLAN

"For I know the thoughts and plans that I have for you, says the Lord, thoughts and plans for welfare and peace and not for evil, to give you hope in your final outcome". (Jeremiah 29:11)

God has a plan for every person and His word clearly says it is a good plan. But Satan starts his dirty work early in your life, attempting to pervert and destroy God's good plan. He arranges for all kinds of disappointing, discouraging, hurtful, and frightening events to take place. And often he does a lot of damage.

But no matter how much you have been hurt, God can restore you. If you experienced a bad beginning, do not despair. God is in the business of repair and His repairs are better than new. However His restoration will not happen automatically. You must believe the word of God and fully cooperate with Him during the restoration process. Look to Jesus, the one who loves you unconditionally. He is the Author and Finisher in everything in you and your life.

As for me, I aim to finish the race well. I do not want the end of my time on earth to be arbitrary, but intentional. My end will come after I have fought that good fight of faith and finished the course. I desire to finish like Paul finished. He said with confidence:

"For I am now ready to be offered, and the time of my departure is at hand. I have fought a good fight, I have finished my course, and I have kept the faith:

Henceforth there is laid up for me a crown of righteousness, which the Lord, the righteous judge, shall give me at that day: and not to me only, but unto all them also that love his appearing" (2Timothy 4:6-8). KJV

Nuggets...Along the Way

RESOURCE PAGE

*Battered wife syndrome is a symptom complex of physical and psychological abuse of a woman by her husband. Such women often present with vague somatic complaints, such as headache, insomnia and abdominal pain. Thus, the diagnosis can usually only be made by asking nonthreatening open-ended questions. Most women remain with their husbands because they are afraid of them. Hence, successful treatment usually depends on the woman's leaving her husband and obtaining help in the development of a new self-concept. (R.W Swanson; PubMed Central Vol.130).

The syndrome develops in response to a three-stage cycle found in domestic violence situations. First, tension builds in the relationship. Second, the abusive partner releases tension via violence whilst blaming the victim for having caused the violence. Third, the violent partner makes gestures of contrition. However, the partner does not find solutions to avoid another phase of tension building and release so the cycle repeats. The repetition of the violence despite the abusers attempts to "make nice" results in the abused partner feeling at fault for not preventing a repeat cycle of violence. However since she is not at fault and the violence is internally driven by the abuser's need to control, this self-blame results in feelings of helplessness rather than empowerment. The feeling of being both responsible for and helpless to stop the violence leads in turn to depression and passivity. This learned depression and passivity make it difficult for the abused partner to marshal the resources and support system needed to leave. (Wikipedia -Walker 1979)

The battered wife syndrome brings to mind the **"can't see the forest for the trees"** saying.

When you're in among the trees, you can't see the forest, and when you're in among the **battered wife issues**, you can't see the syndrome. If you can't see what's really happening, you will feel trapped and helpless--and you're not.

So, on this page you will learn to identify the trees (issues), so that you can **find your way out** of the forest (syndrome). **Loving and caring for yourself** is the key. You are worthy of respect, and that has to start with self respect. (www.AngerManagementResource.com 2007-2011).

BIOGRAPHY OF
VENORIS PATTEN

Venoris Patten is a unique person who embraces the circumstances of her life, endeavoring to see the true purpose of each occurrence. She has come into this awareness over a period of time as she reflected on the journey of her entire life and started questioning the purpose of certain events.

She is the fourth of ten siblings and grew up in a traditional home with mom, dad and siblings. She is the proud mother of two sons and five grandchildren.

Venoris earned her nursing diploma at the University of the West Indies Jamaica, West Indies and later achieved her Bachelors and Masters degrees in Health Services Administration at Florida International University, Miami Florida.

Venoris is passionate about encouraging others and works diligently within the Church and lately the neighboring community to give support to others. She believes strongly in one encouraging the other. Over the past year she has started volunteering with America Cancer Society and most recently with Esther's Outreach Ministry, an organization that offers spiritual, emotional and nutritional support to the local community.

Her book, "Nuggets.....along the Way" is her latest accomplishment. Not only is it a literary legacy for her family and especially her children and grandchildren, but it is also her way of sharing her life to a wider audience. She hopes to encourage all to seek purpose because she believes that living a purpose filled life is the key to real freedom and fulfillment.

Proceeds from her book will go towards Outreach to Battered Women and Abused Girls.

Nuggets...Along the Way

Nuggets...Along the Way

www.ingramcontent.com/pod-product-compliance
Lightning Source LLC
Chambersburg PA
CBHW030932090426
42737CB00007B/400